Community Groups Handbook

Maggie Pearse, Jerry Smith

journeyman

in association with

**COMMUNITY
DEVELOPMENT
FOUNDATION**

This edition first published 1990 by
The Journeyman Press, 345 Archway Road, London N6 5AA
and 141 Old Bedford Road, Concord
MA 01742, USA in association with
Community Development Foundation, 60 Highbury Grove,
London N5 2AG

First published in Great Britain by Community Projects
Foundation as Community Groups Handbooks 1977
Reprinted 1980, 1982

British Library Cataloguing in Publication Data
Pearse, Maggie
    Community groups handbook.
    1.   Community action groups. Organisation
    I.   Title II. Smith, Jerry 1948-
    361.8

    ISBN 1-85172-036-7 hb
            1-85172-037-5

Illustrations by Barbara Kaiser
Printed in Great Britain by Billing and Sons Ltd, Worcester

COMMUNITY GROUPS HANDBOOK

Community Development Foundation

The Community Development Foundation (CDF) (formerly known as the Community Projects Foundation) was set up in 1968 to pioneer new forms of community development.

CDF's role is to show how to involve people in the regeneration of their communities, through a broad programme which includes consultancies, training, local action projects, publications, conferences and research. CDF aims to demonstrate the most effective ways to:

- help people participate in community action and public affairs;
- increase the sensitivity of public authorities to local needs and hopes;
- develop working partnerships between public and private agencies and community groups;
- bring about public policies that regenerate community life.

Chairman: Alan Haselhurst, MP
Chief Executive: David N. Thomas

Registered Charity Number 306130

Contents

Preface to the Second Edition

The original *Community Groups Handbooks* (a set of five) were first published in 1977. They drew on the experience of community activists in the 1970s to produce practical guidelines which have been used by thousands of workers since.

Continuing demand for these books is a tribute to the enduring relevance of basic community work practice, despite changes in legislation, social conditions and political debates. Independent local community organisations are still the main and most effective way by which people participate in public affairs.

But the world has moved on and it was apparent that the Handbooks were becoming out of date. Much of the material on local government had become inaccurate, and the original Handbooks did not refer to a new set of public and private sector organisations which community work now has to deal with. It was necessary to update all this material. We have also added a discussion of community development and race in this revised version to complement the section on women and community development.

The original Handbooks derived from interviews with members of community groups in CDF project areas. We would like to record once more our appreciation of the time and valuable insights they gave us. We felt that this interview material is still as valid today as it was then. The issues about group organisation, tactics, personal development and power which they raise are still with us. Perhaps they always will be.

Maggie Pearse, Jerry Smith

Part 1

How Community Groups Work

Introduction

In this Part we look first of all at the distinctions which can be made between different types of group. We then go on to view the internal workings of community groups in terms of their membership, questions of leadership, the purpose of meetings and how they are run, key jobs within the group and the ways in which groups and wider communities can be organised.

All these are necessary in order to understand how groups keep themselves going. If something is wrong with the way a group works, it has much less chance of achieving its aims, so it is vital to keep an eye on what is happening inside it.

It is easy to blame whatever is wrong on individuals, but when the same situations crop up in different kinds of group in different parts of the country, it cannot be individual personalities which cause the problems. Problems in groups are usually caused by bad systems, not by bad people.

Many people involved in community groups were interviewed for their views, and their experiences highlight the issues raised throughout the book.

Different Types of Groups

Community groups are of various kinds, depending on their aims. We have highlighted eight different types of group but we are concerned mainly with the first six. This is because they are the ones usually involved in trying to change things, whereas the last two - traditional organisations and social groups - are important in a wider sense since they involve people who may take no other part in community activities. All eight types rely on volunteers.

Self-Help Groups exist quite simply to help their members. They are run by the people who benefit from them. Examples are tenant co-operatives, senior citizens groups and parent and toddler groups.

Welfare Groups provide a service for other people. Examples include neighbourhood watch schemes, health groups or advice centres.

Representative Groups are elected by and answerable to the community. They try to respond to what the majority of people want. Tenants and residents associations, and neighbourhood councils fall into this category.

Minority Interest Groups are often self-help groups but also try to improve the rights of certain sections of the population through education and political action. Two examples of such groups are single mothers and black groups.

Action Groups (or Pressure Groups) are self appointed and take action in what they see to be the interests of the whole community. Not being elected, they need to show they have public support in other ways, for instance through petitions or demonstrations. Day nursery and anti-motorway campaigns are good examples.

Liaison Groups are only partly community groups because part of each one is the body with which it is liaising. Such groups are often started by local authorities anxious to improve public participation, for instance between council tenants and the housing department.

Social groups put on social events

Voluntary Organisations are often well-established groups usually catering for a particular sector of the community. Examples include church organisations, Women's Institutes, Boy Scouts and Working Men's Clubs. Such groups often play a big part in the welfare of the community, as well as providing social facilities for their members.

Social Groups exist solely to put on social events. They range from loose groups of neighbours who organise an annual trip to Blackpool, to quite large festival committees, sports leagues and associations for various hobbies.

These are only rough definitions of the different types of community group. In fact, many groups fall into more than one category because they have more than one function. For instance, a group of single mothers may be campaigning to stop landlords discriminating against them, but they may also be helping with each other's children. This means that they are both a minority interest group and a self-help group. Most groups often have both social and educational functions, as well as the action they undertake. Groups also change. An action committee may start with a few people getting together to save their homes from demolition. They may find that all their neighbours agree and that they have become a bigger, more public group with members elected at meetings - in other words, a representative group. This group might eventually take on a welfare function.

Membership

Quantity Versus Quality

No one can give a pat answer as to how large any particular group should be. This depends on its type and what it does. In general, groups running projects, task groups, need more members than action or pressure groups. A task group needs helpers committed to running the project and this usually means a lot of involvement. A pressure group needs a lot of support but the actual work can be done by a few active individuals.

It is vital for groups to have people involved at different levels. Not everyone has the same skills, nor can everyone devote the same amount of time to a group. A good example of this can be seen in the way a community newspaper is produced. The paper can be put together and kept going internally by a handful of people, but they will rely on a larger group to write articles for it, and an even larger group still to distribute it.

A big group is not always more representative than a small one, nor is it always more effective. It's fine to field a team of eleven on a football pitch, but on a tennis court they'd get in each other's way. Quality may be more important than quantity:

> 'Since the first AGM [Annual General Meeting] more people joined, but we've got rid of the dead wood, the people who just came along to see what they could get out of it, and were left with the ones who are really committed.'

If a group has a clear purpose, only people committed to that purpose are likely to join:

> 'We've been fortunate in that no-one we wouldn't have wanted has joined. This is because people realise the work involved.'

Leadership

Many of the people we interviewed saw leadership and Chairing as one and the same, though some recognised that if leaders did emerge they did not necessarily want to be the Chair. Often, Chairs feel they have to lead when they don't want to:

> 'Dave [the Chair] tried to be the leader in the early days - it was forced on him. But Tony was the real leader, efficient and pushing.'

In general, the people we spoke to hadn't given much thought to the question of leadership. A good leader was assumed to be a superhuman character:

> 'Ideally, a committee needs a sparkling, dynamic leader. Someone who's a good listener and gets enthusiastic, is also willing to change his views, has a sense of humour, doesn't follow red herrings and can call the meeting to order with tact.'

The problem of leadership in groups becomes much simpler if it is accepted that leadership involves several different qualities, and therefore there doesn't have to be one leader. It is important to have a cross-section of types of people involved.

The Chair is, or should be, one kind of leader, as he or she is responsible for the conduct of meetings, which are a vital part of the group's life. We look at the Chair's job in more detail later. Another kind of leader is the organiser - the energetic person who pushes the group

along. Being the spokesperson for a group - representing it in public - is another form of leadership. Some people are full of ideas and imaginative schemes: the ideas person is yet another kind of leader. Finally, there are tacticians - people who are concerned with the 'who' and 'how' rather than the 'what' of the group's work.

An organiser

It should be obvious by now that a group will probably have more than one leader. If it doesn't, then it is probably because one person in the group sees him or herself as 'being in charge' and is actually stopping others from using their talents to the full.

Inner Circles

Most groups, including very successful ones, have an 'inner circle' of people who run the show. This can present problems as outsiders may think the group is just a small clique and newcomers, or possibly even people who have been on the fringes of the group for some time, often feel they are being excluded and are not wanted. The inner circle all too often becomes the vicious circle.

The clique will not delegate work. Others feel left out. They do not know how to join in. The inner circle feels 'put upon'. They feel they have been left to carry everything on their shoulders, and they feel it is hopeless to ask anyone to help because they have previously seemed uninterested. It is therefore important that all members are aware of what is going on and that their opinions are taken into account.

Turnover

If all members of the group are made to feel involved, there is less likelihood of groups suffering from a rapid and damaging turnover of membership. Turnover of membership does not automatically mean that there is something wrong with a group. Some groups, like parent and toddler groups, have turnover built into them as toddlers grow up and move on to playgroup or nursery school. Some campaigns and projects need to have people they can rely on at certain times but whom they can afford to let go when things are slack. Groups themselves need to look at the reasons why members are falling by the wayside, and think seriously about ways of putting things right.

Awkward Customers

Groups can attract 'awkward customers' who often have personal problems like loneliness, or a desire to dominate:

> 'Look at the bloke who ran it (a community newspaper) - he acted like the whole thing belonged to him.'

Some awkward customers may have genuine complaints:

> 'One lady turned up and all she could say was that her kitchen sink was bunged up. It was nothing to do with the meeting, but the whole evening was taken up with it.'

Group members must not be afraid to tell such people to stick to the point, and then give them a hearing later at a more appropriate time. Some people have pet subjects that they are obsessed with:

> 'We have one waffler who gets a bee in his bonnet. If he would sit down and shut up it could get dealt with easily, but he won't. He's like a dog with a bone.'

Characters like these often put little into a group, but take up too much of its time. If the group spends a lot of time listening to them, or arguing with them, it only increases their sense of self importance and actually encourages them to carry on. Hard though it may be, the only way to deal with difficult characters is to give them less attention. Above all, dealing with them is the responsibility of the whole group. Too often it is all left to the Chair.

Meetings

Although meetings are often criticised, they are an important part of being a group, rather than just a collection of individuals. Many people can't see the point of meetings. Some may complain that there are too many:

'There were too many meetings and some people just used them for gossiping and passing the time of day.'

Others feel they go on too long. Above all, they complain that meetings stop them from doing more important things:

'People get fed up at meetings because there's too much talking and not enough action.'

Purpose of Meetings

Of course, it helps if members of the group realise the reason for specific meetings, but there are some underlying purposes, common to most meetings, which we want to look at now. Communication is an important factor:

'A lot won't come to meetings. When they don't come, they lose touch.'

Some people get too much attention

In this sense, meetings serve the purpose not only of allowing information to be shared, but also of enabling people to learn to act together as a group and to develop a sense of belonging.

Meetings should control the membership by ensuring that individuals do what the group wants, for the benefit of the group as a whole. When this does not happen meetings are seen as a waste of time.

Three things are essential to this type of control over group members: decisions must be taken; they must be put into practice; and they must be reported back to the group, so that it can judge results. These things will happen only if groups are run well.

Groups must deal with the problem of finding a happy medium between business and socialising. Some hold their meetings in pubs. Others set a time limit on business, leaving time for a chat later on. Others organise social evenings, so that members can enjoy themselves and get to know each other better. If there is a golden rule, it is to keep the business side separate from the social side, but remember that both are important.

How Often?

A guide to how often a group should meet lies in its members and its work. However, the task of deciding how often should become clearer if the group looks at the amount of communications, control and socialising necessary (and indeed desirable) to make meetings work.

Generally, groups with few members, who see each other regularly between meetings, will need fewer meetings than larger groups or ones whose members rarely see each other outside meetings.

How regularly a group should meet is another area which needs to be given some thought. One group member believed:

'It would be fatal to have regular meetings, just for the sake of them. People would get disheartened and we'd lose members.'

In this particular case he was probably right. The group he was in was negotiating with planners about traffic schemes. In such a group there are bound to be slack periods, when the group can do little other than wait for a response from the town hall. Equally, there will be busy times when frequent meetings will be necessary. The main advantage of having regular meetings is that everyone knows when they are. If a group meets only when strictly necessary, a lot of responsibility and trust rests on whoever has the job of calling the meetings.

Organising Meetings

Most meetings need an Agenda: they make the Chair's job easier and speed up the business. It is best for the Chair and Secretary to get together to prepare the Agenda, though any member of the group should have the right to include items for discussion. If your group can't make copies of the agenda for everyone, then it is important that it is clearly displayed (for example on a blackboard or large sheet of paper) during the meeting.

Minutes can range from a simple record of decisions to a full account of all the arguments used and points raised. The latter is only possible using shorthand and is rarely necessary. One Secretary told us that she tried to give the feeling of the meetings - and that's a sensible aim. It is important though, to note not only what decisions were taken but whose job it was to carry out each decision. If the Secretary is not clear at any point on what has been agreed, he or she must ask. It is very likely that others will be confused, too.

Getting Involved

Why Do People Get Involved?

Why is it then, that people become involved in community action? For a few, involvement may well be a part of a wider political or religious conviction which spurs them on to help others. Some undoubtedly become involved because they have a vision of what their neighbourhood could be like if only people cared about it. Many become involved because they realise they have a need or problem in common with other people in the area and they believe that they will have a greater chance of success working with others.

There are many reasons why people get involved with community groups in the first place. A great many people become involved quite by chance and develop strong social commitments a bit later. There are, however, six main ways in which most people get involved with community groups.

Going Along With a Friend

'Barbara next door was involved and she asked me if I wanted my little girl in the playgroup and I was interested. Then I went to the first open meeting and someone put my name forward to go on the committee.'

Owing Someone a Favour

'I've always been one for fighting my own battles but I'd had so many problems with Stockton Street [the local Social Security office], I thought oh, blow it. I'll go to the advice centre and see if they can do something. Pat [the advice centre worker] mentioned something about the adventure playground and asked me to lend a hand at the playscheme. If I hadn't been asked I wouldn't have volunteered.'

Being Forced

'To tell you the truth I had my arm twisted. Lynne was round here one day and she asked whether we knew anything about accounts and I showed her how to draw up a balance sheet. The next meeting we went to I was proposed as Treasurer.'

Starting With Something Small That Develops Into Something Bigger

'When I first started I didn't realise that it would be anything like it is. So many meetings - your involvement just snowballs. I didn't really think much about what it would lead to. I went around doing the door-knocking for the first meeting and I thought that we'd then go to the Town Hall and kick up a fuss and that would be the end of it.'

Feeling Bored, Lonely or Lost in a New Area

'I had come to live with my mam and someone asked me if I wanted to come to a parent and toddler group. I was bored stiff so I went along. It was really boredom that started me on the path to helping people.'

Seeing Something in it for Themselves

'I thought it would be a good idea to get the kids occupied during the holidays - with eight of our own it would be in our own interests if nobody else's! I've never considered myself as a social worker or anything. Just a father of eight kids who wanted to bring them up well.'

Small issues can get bigger

These reasons may seem trivial and they are certainly very personal but they are all valid. You should never deny that you are trying to get some benefit for yourself out of community action. The benefit might be a better house, or a playground for your own kids. It might be a chance to meet new friends, or develop new interests. It might be the satisfaction of doing something useful. Whatever the initial reason, once you join together in a group and try to get the same benefits for other people, then it's no longer a question of being selfish.

Of course, occasionally people become involved in community action for dubious reasons. Some people join community groups because it makes them feel big or successful, whereas at work or at home they may see themselves as failures. If this happens, it needs very careful and sympathetic handling. Such people need help rather than rejection. If they become over-involved this could actually do them harm in the long run, as they may find it difficult to cope with the pressures. Also, the involvement of such a person could harm the group and ultimately the whole community if the group itself does not handle the situation carefully.

In spite of all the different reasons given for getting involved, there are some common threads. It is widely believed that helping oneself is better than being helped; that if you've gone through problems of your own, you can be of more use to people; and that small-scale local changes are just as important as changes at the top. As a justification of community action, that will do for a start, but communication with other groups is also vital.

Why Don't People Get Involved?

If we ask why people get involved, it also makes sense to ask why other people don't get involved. We've seen that many people who do become involved often do so by chance and for fairly ordinary reasons. From interviews with non-involved people it became obvious that it wasn't just laziness or selfishness that stopped them joining in. They gave a number of reasons which need to be examined by anyone interested in attracting new people into community groups. Sometimes there are good reasons for not getting involved.

People may not like what the group is doing or the way it is doing it. They may feel they are not good enough or capable enough to join in; quite simply they may not have been asked. Many activists put people off by being so enthusiastic that other people assume involvement will mean having no time for anything else. Also groups sometimes appear to have everything in hand so that people feel there is little point in offering to help.

Some people attempt to get involved, but drop out quickly because they don't think they have been made welcome. It is important not only to involve people in work, but to involve them socially as well.

In our society we are generally not encouraged to join forces in an effort to help others. In fact, quite the reverse. We are encouraged, at school and at work, to look after ourselves and better ourselves at the expense of others. We are persuaded by TV adverts to spend money on things we don't particularly want, so as to be one better than the Jones's.

Working people have very little leisure time, and may wish to spend what free time they have on hobbies or just relaxing. It's surprising and encouraging that so many people do get involved.

Early Experiences

There are several ways of joining groups. It is easiest when the group itself is new: other people join at the same time as you; you already know people in the group, particularly if you have been brought in by a friend; or you have been asked to help out in a specific way.

The easiest meetings to go to are public meetings: there's safety in numbers and you're less likely to be seen as making a definite commitment. At the other extreme, it is very difficult to join a small group which has existed for some time and where everyone knows one another but you don't know anyone. This is even worse if the group has no clear idea of what it expects from you.

Most people we talked to about their early experiences had not found it easy. They spoke of being asked to give far more than they'd intended; of being ignored; of being overawed by technical terms; of not understanding the rules or the way the group worked; and of being afraid to open their mouths in case they were shouted down.

'Some disliked the meetings, either because they were badly run or because they preferred practical work to talking. Nearly all were very nervous at first. One woman told of how she never opened her mouth or raised her eyes from the floor for six months until one day someone said something with which she disagreed so strongly that, in spite of herself, she found herself on her feet arguing with him. She hasn't looked back since.'

Though it doesn't usually happen in such a spectacular way, most of those who stuck at it did find their self-confidence increasing. In fact, increased self-confidence was generally rated as one of the most important gains.

However, for every person who stays the course, several more will probably drop out in the early stages. We have already hinted at why this happens and we want now to look at some of these reasons more closely.

Effects on People

Community action involves ordinary people, and community activists are, by and large, a good cross-section of the people in the area. But the very fact that these ordinary people become involved changes things. It changes their attitudes and ideas:

'It's changed my outlook on life a great deal. It's made me less class-conscious, I think. Too many people think anyone on Social Security is somehow less of a human being ... and I've realised this isn't true.'

They become more self-confident:

'Previously, I'd had a bit of an inferiority complex about my situation - lots of kids and no husband. Now all of a sudden people liked me, and I found most of them had liked me all along.'

'I've learned a lot personally from the playgroup about how to be with my child. I've learned how to play with her and not to restrict her.'

However, changes are not always positive and people reported mixed views from their friends about their involvement, ranging from friends thinking they were doing a wonderful job to the view that they were only doing it in order to look big. Others had friends who they thought were a little jealous:

'Some friends think you're mad and some admire you for knowing things. Some people think you should have better things to do with your time, like being at home. Maybe they're resentful that you've got something to do and they haven't.'

Although some people lost friends through spending too little time with them, most felt their involvement had improved their home life and social life.

Feeling Involved

A group which has been together for some time is likely to develop its own style, customs, catch phrases and even standing jokes and this can be off-putting to a newcomer who will not readily understand what is really going on. It is surprising how quickly a group can get into a rut, with set assumptions and a rigid approach to the way things are tackled. These ideas may seem obscure or wrong to a new member, but the old hands might not like the thought of a challenge, even if they admit privately that their system is not working too well.

You can attend meetings for months without ever feeling part of the group. You may keep on going because you believe the group is worthwhile but sooner or later (and probably sooner) you'll need something more.

The feeling of involvement, the feeling that you are important to the group and that in its turn the group gives you something, can come in various ways. The woman mentioned before got hers from arguing a point in a meeting; if you contribute to a discussion and know that the group has taken your point seriously (even if the majority disagree) then you are likely to feel part of the group.

Doing something on behalf of the group can also help you to feel involved. One activist emphasised the importance of learning by doing:

> 'You have to tell people:"It comes with experience, not text-books. Come in and watch others, then try it and that's the way to learn."'

Another said:

> 'Personally, I'm not one for meetings. I got involved in the voluntary wardens scheme because it was a way of doing something on the estate without going to meetings. There are definitely a lot of others who feel the same way. You'd get more response if you organised things that didn't need meetings.'

But some groups are, by nature, less involved in practical work. Often such groups have been set up to fight a threat - a rent rise or a road scheme for instance - or to pressure the authorities to do more for the area. The feeling of involvement in these groups is usually that of fighting for a just cause. The knowledge that what you and the group are doing is right and important is perhaps the strongest commitment of all. Another way in which people come to feel involved is through making friends in the group:

> 'I've met a lot of new people. Although we'd been here four years we knew very few people before, only really the neighbours on either side.'

On balance the experiences of the people we interviewed suggest that in some way or other this feeling of involvement does come along in the end, for those who can stick to it for long enough.

Taking Part

Let's assume that you've just joined or are about to join a community group; that you've been persuaded into joining it, that you only have a vague idea of what the group does and no idea how it works; you don't know most of the people in the group; the first meeting seems to be getting nowhere; and you're afraid to open your mouth because you don't yet know the rules of the game. What should you do?

People get involved at different levels

You need to take a look at yourself. First, what do you want to achieve? Are you interested mainly in helping others, standing up for your rights, changing people's attitudes, battling with officialdom - or what? Knowing your own motives will help you to decide whether you want to stay in the group and, if so, what part you want to play in it.

The other thing you need to know about yourself is what skills you have. That doesn't necessarily mean whether you can type, or draw, or Chair meetings, useful as these things are. At bottom it means what kind of a person you are. What particular interests do you have - children, the elderly, housing, transport for example? Could you bring in other people to the group? Are you friendly with people whose help or support the group could use, such as councillors? Do you have time on your hands? Everyone has something to offer.

You need to take a look at the group. For some, this means constantly asking questions. For others, it means lying low for a while and working things out in your own mind - it depends on how you learn best. In any event, you'll need to find out what the group's aims are, what it has achieved so far and where it has failed; who does what in the meetings;

and whether things go on behind the scenes (this isn't necessarily a bad thing). Try to see this first stage - it may take a couple of weeks or several months - as a trial period. If necessary, make it clear to the group that you want time to decide before committing yourself too far.

The main thing is to decide whether you want to be part of the group and, if so, in what capacity. You may decide to leave but, if so, it will be for good reasons and not for those discussed earlier. Of course, the answer may be that you should stay with the group and try to alter it. Obviously, you need to think carefully before you decide to remain in a group. If the changes you have in mind are major ones, they could be inappropriate and this could mean you've joined the wrong group in the first place. For example, if you're interested in housing and the group has been set up to provide playschemes, you should try to find a housing group - or even start one with others who share your interest. On the other hand, if your objection is that the group tackles issues in the wrong way, then there's no reason why you shouldn't stay with it and share your ideas with the rest of the group.

Staying In and Dropping Out

A once-prominent member of a community association who had left the group said:

> 'I got disillusioned. Lots of petty reasons. Meetings went on too long, there was a lot of unrest; the community had become split; nobody was taking any notice of the community workers; people were being overworked. Small reasons, but they added up. And there was a personal reason too.'

This quote reflects the four main reasons we found for people giving up: disillusionment; disagreements within the group; uneven division of work; and personal reasons and pressure at home. It's worth looking more closely at how these might be avoided.

Disillusionment

You don't become disillusioned, of course, unless you begin with illusions. Two kinds of illusions are common. The first is to imagine that the mere existence of a group will in itself cause something to change. It is true that new groups often do have an initial run of success without having to try very hard. This may be because beginners often use surprise tactics which pay off or because the authorities overestimate the group's strength or, perhaps more likely, because the authorities calculate that giving in to a few demands at the start will make the group compromise over its bigger aims. Whatever the reason, success in the long term is by no means assured. If you begin with the idea that the group only has to blow its trumpet for the walls to come down, you're sure to be disappointed. So don't blame the group for not achieving something that was unrealistic in the first place.

The other illusion is that your fellow members in the group should be pillars of the community, a class apart. It's more than likely they'll have about as many strengths and weaknesses as you have. If you expect more from them you're again heading for disappointment. This is not to deny that there are some remarkable people about. Above all though, what counts is how the group works together, not the individual personalities.

Disagreements in the Group

Disagreements occur in every group. Often arguments are a healthy sign, indicating that people are enthusiastic and committed to what they are doing. If disagreements rarely occur, it may well be because the group has become a cosy social club with little relevance to the community. But in some groups disagreements do run at a level which stops work being done and makes life unpleasant. The disagreements which are really damaging are those which crop up again and again, wasting the group's time. It is important, then, to avoid this first by taking clear majority decisions (voting if necessary) rather than shelving awkward topics, and then by ensuring that everyone abides by those decisions.

The people we spoke to tended to see all disagreements as personality clashes. Although there are some prickly people about, it is unlikely that all or even most conflicts within groups can be put down to personality. A lot of conflicts are real differences of opinion about what should be done or how to do it. Others occur because of genuine misunderstandings. The first step in dealing with disagreements is to look beyond how others say things to what it is they are saying; why they feel this way and where their views come from. Several people emphasised the importance of bringing disputes out into the open:

'We have got a good group, a committee which sticks together, and when we do have disagreements we can beat problems out together and talk about them.'

As for the prickly people, we've said already that a few do become involved for the wrong reasons and can damage both the group and themselves in the process. Such people, as one activist pointed out, are unlikely to leave the group because their status in it means so much to them.

People get involved who aren't clear what they want, they often can't make a success of their own lives, and being in a group is the most important thing for them. By staying on they become a big fish in a small pool and they're very hard to get out. In the end this may drive out other people because they can always find something else to do.

Many good people do indeed drop out because of this. What is really needed is for the rest of the group to make an effort to bring the awkward person into line. That may not sound very nice, but it's what would happen in a situation you couldn't just walk out of - at work for instance. If this fails, then the group must be prepared in the end to tell the person to go. Forcing an awkward person out, though it may be distasteful, is better than losing good people.

Sharing the Work Load

There are three main pitfalls to be avoided in the way a group copes with dividing up its tasks.

It is easy to take on too much work and this can have adverse effects, not only on the person involved and the group as a whole, but also on home life. As one woman said:

'Because I've been so involved I haven't really been managing at home and I need to cut down somewhere. It's very easy to get more involved than you intended to. You need to think carefully about what is important and what you are doing, otherwise your home life suffers.'

So it's always worth thinking carefully and making priorities before taking on something which could be done better by someone else, with less to do or more time than you.

Underwork can be just as bad as overwork. Sometimes new members feel undervalued because they are given no work to do. They begin to wonder what they are doing in the group and to feel they are wasting their time. As we have already said, having something practical to do is one of the ways in which people become truly involved in the group.

Groups tend to rely on a core of trusted members - usually long standing - to do the important jobs. New members are often given the run-of-the-mill, tedious jobs but if this practice continues they may begin to feel undervalued, exploited and like a general dogsbody. To some extent, newcomers should expect to serve an apprenticeship but the point here is that you are supposed to learn and take on more and more responsibility:

> 'New members should be brought in gradually and worked through a steady process till they become self-confident, then they should be given responsibility.'

The more evenly a group shares out the work to be done, the more democratic it is likely to be. The best decisions are made by people who know from practical experience what they are talking about. If all the work is done by two or three people, they will tend to be the ones who make the decisions, since no one else will have the know-how.

Pressure at Home

Many people find resistance at home to their becoming active in the community. This affects women in particular, as a lot of men still believe that women belong in the home. Those with children have the added practical problem of finding baby-sitters in order to attend meetings, although this ought not to be so. Men may be threatened about their partner's involvement. As one woman said:

> 'Me and him have nearly murdered each other - he says I should go off to the bloody project then. '

Similarly, a wife may be dismayed to find her husband is spending a lot of time away from home because of his involvement:

> 'We had a lot of rows about me spending too much time away. Norma couldn't see the point of it. She thought people should just look after themselves and couldn't understand why I was always out helping everyone else and neglecting the family. We did manage to compromise a bit. I cut down on the work and she started visiting one or two old people.'

While there are no easy answers to home pressures, we can at least make some practical suggestions about minding children. The group could organise a baby-sitting rota, or there may be one already in the area, perhaps run as part of a parent and toddler group. For daytime meetings a creche - a room where children under school age can be looked after - could be organised. This, too, could be done on a rota basis, or perhaps people not involved in the group itself might be able to help out in this way. If these can't be arranged, a babysitting kitty could be organised, to which all members of the group contribute, to pay for babysitters for those who need them. A little bit of practical help is better than a lot of sympathy.

Two suggestions can be made about unsympathetic partners. The first is that other people will certainly have faced the same problems and some may have found ways of overcoming them. By talking to them and using their support, you might find a way out which fits your own situation. The second bit of advice we can give is don't let yourself get into the position of being out at meetings every night, unless you've got an almost saintly partner. Perhaps the best solution, if it can be made to work, is a compromise. Persuade your partner to show some interest in the community in return for cutting down on your own commitment. If he or she sees at first hand what you are doing, there will be more understanding and less suspicion or jealousy.

People and Jobs

In order to develop the theme of meetings further and to look in greater detail at how a group works, we will use an imaginary community group as an example. At the end of this section we go on to examine the jobs of key people in a group - the Chair, Secretary and Treasurer.

Using an Agenda

The Chair and Secretary of our imaginary group had got together the week before the meeting to finalise the agenda, which was then typed up and delivered to group members. Spare copies were kept to be given to people who forgot to bring them on the evening.

Monthly meeting of Maple Grove Residents Association

Tuesday 18 November at 8 p.m.

Agenda

1. Apologies for absence
2. Minutes of previous meeting
3. Matters arising from the minutes
4. Correspondence
5. Day Nursery Campaign
6. Housing Repairs
7. Christmas social events
8. Any other business
9. Date of next meeting

The first four items and the last two should always be on the Agenda, so for this meeting, there were three special items for discussion. If a topic is already on the Agenda, it should be dealt with in its right place and not under 'Matters Arising' or 'Correspondence'.

> 'Agendas are far too long. We don't have time to deal with items properly.'

This complaint illustrates the danger of trying to do too much. Three or four items, apart from regular ones, are plenty.

The early routine items should be dealt with as quickly as possible, in order to leave time for the main business. This means that the Chair may need to be fairly strict. Any important letters should be given space as separate items rather than be dealt with under correspondence. This is not always possible though, as the letter may only arrive shortly before the meeting. It is also a good idea to include the most important items first, so that they get a good airing while people's minds are still fresh.

Regular Items (1-4)

At our imaginary meeting, the Chair called the meeting to order when everyone had arrived a little after 8.00 p.m., asked for any apologies for absence (there were two) and noticed that there were two new faces present. She asked their names, welcomed them to the group and introduced the other members. The Minutes of the previous meeting were read out by the Secretary. One person said she had been mis-quoted. This was put right and the Chair signed the Minutes as correct. Two people raised questions under Matters Arising; one wanted to

Bonfire nights can be fun - and profitable

check whether another member had done what he had agreed (he hadn't but had made the arrangements); the Treasurer reported on the small profit made by the party on bonfire night.

The Secretary read out one item of correspondence, a letter from a local resident complaining about a dangerous road and asking the Association to do something about it. The meeting agreed to write to a local councillor about a zebra crossing and to the police about putting a radar trap on the road, and to take the matter further at a later meeting if they had no success. The Chair made sure that someone would call on the woman who wrote the letter to tell her what had been done. This might be a way of involving a new person in the group; in any case it is this kind of attention to detail which keeps a group in touch with its community.

Day Nursery Campaign (5)

The first main agenda item was quite straightforward. A sub-group had been set up two meetings previously to campaign for a day nursery in the area, and had got up a petition, which had been passed on to a local councillor who was also on the Social Services Committee. Two women from this group reported back that they had received a letter from the Director of Social Services saying that on no account could a day nursery be provided because of the spending cuts.

Some members of the group said they weren't surprised and it was stupid to ask for it in the first place. Others pointed out that a day nursery had been promised for ten years and the excuse was always that the money was not yet available. The Chair let the discussion go on until she felt everyone had put their views across and people were beginning to repeat points. Then she asked the group whether they wanted to continue with the campaign and, if so, how? It was agreed that the sub-group first needed to get facts together to support its case (for example how many young children and working women there were in the area). Two members of the sub-group were delegated to get the information, and after this the whole group would need to talk about tactics.

Housing Repairs (6)

The next item was a letter received during the month from the Housing Department, asking the Association for its view on which housing repairs should receive priority for the council tenants in the area. About half the houses in Maple Grove were council houses but there was no separate council tenants association. Immediately some of the council tenants started making suggestions. One woman raised a repair problem of her own, but the Chair ruled that this should be dealt with under any other business and the group should stick to general questions here. Someone suggested that the group should have nothing to do with the request since asking tenants to make priorities was an excuse for reducing the amount of repairs carried out. Another disagreed strongly, saying that this was an opportunity to put tenants' views across and it should not be missed. In view of the strength of feelings on the matter,

Housing repairs ...

and aware that the Association did not just include council tenants, the Chair suggested that they organise a public meeting for tenants as soon as possible and ask the housing manager to attend. This was agreed, with a few people against the idea. The Chair and the Secretary offered to organise the meeting, but all members were asked to help with leafleting and other publicity.

Christmas Social Events (7)

Last year the group ran two Christmas parties - one for children and one for OAPs. It was quickly agreed to do the same this year. A sub-group was elected to do the organising; it included the two new members (practical projects are often the best way of involving newcomers) and two other volunteers. It was also agreed to ask one of the two absentee members to help, as she had been involved last year and knew the ropes. This was a good idea - people who can't attend a meeting shouldn't be excluded from the group's activity. The Chair made sure that the sub-group's rights and responsibilities were clear; they had a free hand to do as they liked, provided they didn't spend more than £50, and were to report back at the first meeting after Christmas. All members were urged to help out on the day.

Regular Items (8-9)

Under 'Any Other Business' the council tenant already mentioned asked the group to take up her housing complaint. The group had already received several other complaints and the Secretary agreed to write to the housing department about them. The next meeting was fixed for 16 December but, as this was near Christmas, it would be mainly a social meeting and only urgent business would be dealt with. The meeting ended at 9.30 p.m.

Points to Note

We deliberately chose a very broad group (a residents association) for our imaginary example. Such a group covers a bigger range of topics than most other community groups. Also, we illustrated an ideal meeting and most won't run so smoothly. We should stress that the account just given is not meant to be the Minutes of the meeting, which would not need to be nearly as full. However, we have highlighted many of the things a Chair has to do and, most importantly, that all members of the group need to be involved in the meeting.

The Chair

During the course of our imaginary meeting, the Chair:

- called the meeting to order when she felt it was time to make a start;
- asked for apologies for absence;
- welcomed and involved new members;
- signed the approved Minutes of the previous meeting;
- saw to it that the Agenda was followed and that matters were raised at the right time;
- cut off the discussion when she felt it had gone on long enough;

The Chair needs to keep control of meetings

- made suggestions about how the group should deal with Agenda items;
- offered her help as a member of the group;
- expressed her own views;
- encouraged others to express theirs;
- made sure that the responsibilities for taking action were clear;
- ensured a date was fixed for the next meeting;
- declared the meeting closed.

This covers a great deal of what the Chair should do in meetings. In between, he or she needs to keep in close touch with any sub-groups appointed to do particular jobs.

The thorniest aspect of the Chair's job is keeping control in the meetings. The Chair needs to know (or sense) when a discussion has gone on long enough and needs to be brought to a close. Cutting off a topic, when others want to continue, is bad but letting two people go over the same arguments for an hour, boring everyone else silly, is probably worse. The Chair also needs to know when a group has reached consensus (agreement) and when a vote needs to be taken. Votes aren't often necessary in the fairly informal atmosphere of community groups, but they can be useful as a way of making it crystal clear to a minority that a minority is exactly what they are. Votes are also needed for electing officers, of course.

Expecting Too Much of the Chair

Most people tend to think the Chair should run the meetings, but this attitude fails to take into account the fact that the whole group is really responsible for the conduct of the meeting. The Chair should be able to expect the active support of the group, provided he or she is doing what the group wants.

The Chair is not a thought-reader and cannot do the job of controlling the meeting entirely alone. Members should say if they feel the meetings are run badly. During the meetings they should help the Chair, for example by suggesting that a discussion be put to a vote. Given helpful suggestions from members, the Chair is far more likely to do a good job.

The Chair and Power

If too much pressure is put upon Chairs, they either crack up or resign, but some Chairs actually enjoy the responsibility, because of the power that goes with it. If the members do not involve themselves in the running of meetings, the Chair is left entirely in charge - and may become a little dictator because of this. Some groups try to share out the responsibilities and the power of the Chair by rotating the job - having a different person take it in turns at each meeting. However this solution may not work:

'Having a rotating Chair doesn't work. No one calls the meetings. Often the person who's supposed to be Chair fails to turn up and there's no continuity.'

This shows that if the Chair is to rotate, the group must be exceptionally well organised. At the other extreme are groups whose Chairs have served for years, either because no one else is prepared to or because other people who might stand are put off:

'The Chair keeps saying he'll resign, but he never does. A couple of years ago we had found someone else to take over, but at the AGM someone proposed the old Chair, who said he didn't really want to stand, but if people really wanted him to... He declared himself elected without a vote.'

The job of Chair probably does need continuity, but it also needs new blood from time to time.

The Secretary

The Secretary's job tends to be less perilous than that of Chair but it may involve more work. The main work of the Secretary is:

- taking the Minutes of meetings;
- distributing copies of the Minutes to members or reading out the Minutes at the next meeting, for approval;
- distributing reminders of meetings to members (possibly with the Agenda);
- writing letters on behalf of the group;
- keeping copies of letters written and received;
- reading out correspondence at meetings.

The Secretary may also be responsible for keeping the membership informed, through a newsletter, of what the group is doing. This is particularly true in representative organisations with a large number of paid-up members, comparatively few of whom attend meetings. If a group has either a great deal of correspondence or needs to produce a regular newsletter for its members, it may wish to split up the job of Secretary and add a Minutes Secretary, who deals with Agendas and Minutes, leaving the Secretary free to take care of the correspondence and communicate with the membership.

Being the Secretary of a group does not mean that you have to do everything on the secretarial side, but the day-to-day organisation of things is not easy.

Of course, it is easy for a Secretary to get overloaded with work and there is no reason why tasks shouldn't be undertaken by other members of the group. As one Secretary said:

'The Chair and I share tasks, together with another member and I'd say the three of us play the most active roles in the group. The Chair's partner and one other member play supporting roles - making decisions and helping with jobs, when necessary.'

The weight of correspondence varies from group to group, but all groups need someone who can write letters. The style of writing, and

Secretaries often get overloaded with work

even things like spelling and punctuation, are quite important, but more important is that what is being said is clear. A neatly laid-out, accurately spelt letter gives the impression of a well-run group, but equally a less professional-looking letter often hits home. Above all, write in your own language - don't attempt to imitate the language and jargon of bureaucrats. Unless you can do it very well, they'll only laugh. It helps a lot if the Secretary can type, since copies of important letters should be kept and this is time-consuming if it means copying out in longhand.

The Secretary and Chair need to work closely together, both in preparing meetings and during them. However, the combination of Chair and Secretary can be a powerful one and they should not only be able to co-operate but also to act as a brake on one another. Otherwise they may well become the inner circle of the group and, as we've seen, this can be dangerous. On the other hand, sometimes a strong Secretary and Chair can keep a group alive.

> 'In the past, people were unreliable and forgot to do things. We two - I know it sounds terrible - were the most reliable and we kept the group going, so people trusted us and began to show interest again.'

Providing there are good reasons why a group should continue and those involved are aware of the pitfalls, there is nothing wrong in this.

The Treasurer

Handling the group's money is a responsible job, though by no means always a difficult one. There is advice on accounts and bookkeeping in publications produced by many organisations (see Appendix) and we only want to look at more general matters here. Even small amounts of cash give rise to suspicions and many a Treasurer has resigned through unjust accusations (or more usually, veiled hints) that funds have gone astray. There is only one solution, which is to keep the accounts up-to-date and as simple as possible, so that other members of the group can quickly see that they are straight. Accounts should be produced for inspection by any member of the group at any time of the year, but the

The Treasurer looks after the group's money

Treasurer has the right to expect a couple of week's notice, since no one can be expected to have work absolutely up-to-date at all times. Other safeguards are to:

- keep receipts for what has been spent;
- have the accounts audited by outsiders once a year (before the AGM, if the group has one);
- nominate other members (as well as the Treasurer) to sign cheques;
- ensure that any cheque drawn on the group's account has at least two signatures.

One of the biggest headaches a Treasurer has is to account properly for money and grants the group receives from the council or other bodies such as trust funds. Unless your group has an experienced Treasurer it will be important to seek outside help in this situation. Very often the council itself will provide free advice and some councils employ staff to help community groups with accounting. It is worth asking about this, especially if you have a grant from the council. Organisations such as the Action Resource Centre (see Appendix) may have a local community accountancy project in your area which could help.

Beyond this, like all other members of the group, Treasurers have the right to be trusted by others to do their work. Unless groups have a large turnover of money, it is a waste of their time and an insult to the Treasurers if they have to account for every penny spent at each meeting.

Treasurers are important to the success of community groups; if money isn't handled correctly, groups can lose credibility which could be disastrous.

Group Organisation

How organised should a group be? This is difficult to answer as there are strong arguments on both sides. Some people complain of too much organisation:

> 'People receive a wad of information before each Management Committee meeting. It tends to scare people off. I think it could be simplified.'

But others complain of too little organisation:

> 'They never want to run things properly. They don't like writing letters. You can't run a committee like that because you don't know where you are when someone leaves.'

The pros and cons of having a formal, organised group are almost endless and the people we interviewed had a wide range of views on the subject. Nevertheless, a certain amount of organisation is necessary, although it is also important to create a relaxed and friendly atmosphere. The balance between the two will depend on what the group is trying to do and perhaps on the preferences of its members. All the same, it is worth taking a look at the main arguments for and against having a formal group - a group, that is, with firm rules and procedures, and where everyone's responsibilities are spelled out.

Rules and Regulations

Both rules and freedom can be abused. If there are no agreed rules or ways of doing things, the strongest personalities in a group usually run things their way - and there is nothing any of the other members can do about it, short of personal abuse.

The strongest personality usually runs things

On the other hand, if there are too many rules, or the rules are so complicated that only a few old hands know their way around them, these few people can also effectively control things. Some rules or procedures are vital because they:

- are the means by which any member acting against the group's interests can be brought into line;
- are a way of showing members what is expected of them (people usually feel easier when they know this); and
- can be a way of showing the outside world that the group is responsible.

To sum up, it's best to have only rules which are necessary and those you do have should be easily understandable. Above all, they should be general rules, rather than an endless list of nit-picking regulations which is always having additions made to it in the light of each new situation.

Constitutions

A Constitution gives a group legal status and without one a group does not exist in law. It sets out the aims and the objectives of the group and the rules by which it will operate. A Constitution helps to show the outside world that the group is worthy of funds or is politically responsible. By no means do all groups need a Constitution and they are rarely helpful in day-to-day work. Model Constitutions - to be copied or adapted - are available for many kinds of group, such as tenants associations or adventure playground associations.

Division of Labour

If your group has been doing the same things for years, expects to go on doing them and everyone is happy with this, then formal ways of doing business may be the most efficient. Most community groups, however, need to be able to change and respond to outside events. For them a formal organisation can be like a straitjacket so most groups need some freedom to experiment. The main area in which this can be done is the way the group divides up its work.

All groups need some division of labour. If a job is no one person's responsibility, the chances are that it won't get done. Some jobs, like Treasurer, need a consistent approach and cannot be simply rotated around the group on a week-to-week basis. The other argument in favour of division of labour is efficiency: if each aspect of the group's work is the responsibility of one person, that person soon becomes skilled at the job and does it more quickly and better than anyone who is not used to it.

There are dangers too, of course. Individual areas of responsibility can turn into little empires, jealously guarded. People may pursue their own line so single-mindedly that they lose track of what

It's easy to overdo the paperwork

the group as a whole is doing. Having certain skills gives some people power in the group. Secretaries on whom the group has come to depend may constantly threaten to resign if they don't get their own way, for instance. If someone in such a position does leave for any reason, filling the gap left may be very difficult. In a group where all the work is divided up permanently, there is no room for newcomers. All members need the chance to learn about as many aspects of the group's work as possible; most people also like to work as part of a team.

A strict division of labour is best for a group with a very stable membership, doing a job it is used to and expects to have to continue. A more flexible approach is needed for new groups, those with a high turnover of members, or those involved in work which is always changing. Most community groups come in this last category but even they need some permanent division of labour just to keep the wheels turning smoothly.

Paperwork

The other main aspect of organisation is paperwork. All groups should keep records, though it is easily possible to do too much paperwork. A group's records are its memory: they can be used to avoid going over the same ground twice; they can be used to settle many disputes; they guard against people leaving with everything stored in their heads; and they should be an important aid to introducing new members to the group's work. We are not suggesting that every community group installs a roomful of filing cabinets. The essential records are accounts, Minutes of meetings (which need not be long) and copies of important correspondence (including copies of letters the group has sent). It is also useful, if it can be arranged, to record other important events in a diary - an important telephone conversation, perhaps, or a useful piece of information picked up from the radio or TV. Some groups may find a file or scrapbook of newspaper cuttings valuable. However, these extras are not as important as the basic records of meetings and copies of correspondence.

Conclusions

To sum up, organisation in itself is neither good nor bad. What makes it good or bad is the use to which it is put. For instance, there must be rules about how meetings are organised. People should speak through the Chair and not argue among themselves, all talking at once. Suggestions for action must be properly proposed so that everyone knows exactly what they are, who is responsible for what so that they can be recorded in the Minutes.

A group's structure - its rules, procedures and division of labour - should be there to help the group do what it has set out to do. If the structure gets in the way of what the majority want to do, then the structure must be changed. Most community groups need areas of flexibility, as well as rules and division of labour; the groups need to be able to change and individuals within them need opportunities to learn and share one another's work.

How Groups Change

Groups go through certain stages in their lives and change is inevitable. However, groups can become trapped in one stage. Stagnation occurs when the group cannot organise itself to work through its problems, but instead swills them endlessly round and round. Change can cause problems if the reasons for it are not understood. How, then, do groups change?

Early Life

The Secretary of one residents' association said:

'The group was very strong in the early stages - there was more to fight for then.'

Groups of this type are likely to start around an issue about which people feel strongly. There are powerful reasons for the group's existence. People who start groups are also frequently enthusiastic and energetic characters. The group's early life may be chaotic, but there is warmth and friendliness and a sense of purpose.

'In the early days I really thought we were going somewhere and that we'd become a force to be reckoned with.'

Growing Pains

The strength of the group, like a magnet, has the effect of attracting more people to it. New members are drawn in often out of curiosity as much as anything, but the group cannot continue growing forever. Conflicts are likely to develop within it. The founder members may resent seeing their group taken over, or may think the kind of people joining it are not the right sort. Because it has grown so rapidly, the group's organisation will still be primitive, suitable to the small group of friends who started it, but not to a large number of strangers who may not even like one another. The organisation is unable to cope with the conflicts in the group; people become disillusioned and drop out.

Giving Up or Going On?

Meanwhile, the group is busy dealing with the authorities. It may win outright, in which case it has to decide whether to fold up or proceed on another issue. It may run into a brick wall, in which case it has to decide whether to give up or try to find a way around. It may find that no decision can be taken for some time (perhaps years), in which case it has to be prepared for a waiting game. It is very unfair, but a fact, that a group has to take some of its crucial decisions at a very early stage in its life before its members have gained much experience and maybe before they have really got to know one another.

A successful group develops the organisation to take decisions.

Groups can grow, but not forever

Keeping the Wheels Turning

There will also be changes in the group's leadership. The energetic people are still needed, but above all the group now needs level-headed leaders who can cope with a much less exciting stage of its existence. There is hard work such as fact-finding to build up a case. There is sometimes boredom, for instance, when the authorities use delaying tactics or the group has to wait months to hear whether its application for a grant was successful. There may even be no point in the group continuing to meet regularly. You can't sustain action in these groups because by their nature, action in them is going to be spasmodic. Keeping the interest going is the big problem.

Some groups try to solve this by concentrating on social activities. The problem here is that they may end up as nothing more than a social group. This is fine but there will still be issues and someone has to tackle them.

The Need For Change

There are very few examples of groups remaining as campaigning groups for more than a couple of years. There is always a need for new groups to emerge, as old ones become set in their ways, or as issues change. Members of more established groups need to recognise this and encourage others to take action. Sadly, there are those who see anyone else taking an initiative as interference.

Groups inevitably change, then. They change because of internal conflicts, because new members

Some of the fun can go when groups change

bring new ideas and ways of doing things, because the members learn how to work better, and because issues change. New, enthusiastic groups turn into older, organised groups and some of the fun is lost in the process:

'I think those meetings in the first twelve months were great. There was a lot of concern. We were a really friendly group, and we really got into working together. It's changed a lot since then. It's very hard to explain the changes. The whole approach to the work is different. I think it became too professional. The laughter went out of the group.'

Many of the changes are difficult; certainly not all the members will want the group to change. However, the worst groups are those which are unable to change, either because they have no way of working through their difficulties or because they have become so set in their ways that they are unable to respond to the outside world any longer.

Changed circumstances demand new ways of working. Often they demand new people or at least changes in leadership. It is not surprising that most people see changes in the group as due to personality clashes and so on - that's just how it feels on the inside. From outside it can be seen that most groups go through very similar changes, so it can't all be explained by talking about individuals. Once this is understood, group members can cope with the inevitable changes more easily.

Community Organisation

Sub-Committees

As long as we are talking about single groups with clear and specific aims, life is fairly simple. However, very often different groups need to co-operate with one another. Large groups, such as community associations, often split up into sub-committees, and questions about how independent these sub-committees should be may well arise. In this section we look at the different ways in which groups and sub-groups in the community relate to each other.

An Example

Imagine that a new estate has been built and the tenants have moved in. They're quite happy with their new houses and the surroundings, but, after a year or so, some of the roads still haven't been made up, so a couple of neighbours call a public meeting to air this grievance. Councillors promise to get the problem dealt with but someone at the meeting suggests they still need a tenants association to keep an eye open for other difficulties and to foster community spirit.

A committee is elected and a tenants association formed. The committee decides something should be done about the needs of young children on the estate, so it sets up a sub-committee to get a playgroup going. Over the next two years, other sub-committees are started: to look after the elderly, to run a community newspaper, to campaign for a launderette, and to organise social events. The way these groups co-operate with one another, with the main committee and with other community organisations, is an example of the topic we have called community organisation.

The tenants association in our example faces several potential problems. Now there are all these groups, what is there left for the main committee to do? Will all the sub-committees accept that they are responsible to the main committee or will some declare their independence? The launderette campaign may want to use militant tactics but this might upset the old people's sub-committee who want to keep a respectable image. The playgroup and the social committee might be in conflict with each other over premises. Could the tenants association take on a really big fight, such as campaigning about damp throughout the estate?

A large part of the problem stems from having developed a structure of committees and sub-committees, which is not appropriate to the job the tenants association has to do. This often happens early on:

> 'We split up into a lot of sub-groups. A lot of the same people were in different sub-groups and I think it was too much. I don't think we could really handle it. I don't think people really understood it - it was done too quickly.'

We discussed different kind of groups at the beginning of this Part. The

A working party ...

tenants association, as a whole, is a representative organisation but the sub-groups are of three different kinds. The launderette campaign is a pressure group, the old people's committee a care group and the playgroup is probably a bit of both. The social committee might be a care group as well as a social group, but what about the community newspaper, which is a mixture of all these?

A system which puts the central committee or the executive at the top of the pyramid and which asks all these different groups to behave in the same way is doomed to failure. One member of a group commented that:

> 'When we set up the Executive the trouble started. We needed an Executive to keep everything working together, but people didn't like being left out of anything.'

This is hardly surprising. When people have put a lot time and energy into a particular piece of work they don't like others who have not been involved with it taking decisions about how things should proceed. Too often the executive becomes a collection of committee people:

> 'I'm so involved with the different committees that I don't have time to go out and do much of the actual leg work myself.'

This remark highlights the possible danger of losing touch with the community you are meant to represent.

Alternatives

What other kinds of structure could the tenants association in our example adopt? There are several ways in which tenants, residents or community associations can organise themselves to represent the interests of the whole neighbourhood over a range of issues.

Perhaps we should look first at the sub-groups after all as they are where most of the work is done. Some sub-groups will need to be permanent committees, if there is no obvious end point to their job. This would apply, for instance, to the old people's care group.

Over some issues the association would want to keep its options open for a time. It might, for example, want first to look at the needs of the under-fives before deciding whether it could best tackle the problems through campaigning for nursery provision, fundraising to start a playgroup or running its own parents and toddlers club. In this case, the sub-group dealing with the problem should be set up as a working party with very clear terms of reference and, if possible, a date by which it should bring its ideas to the association. The working party would have to discover not only the relevant facts about local needs but also investigate the politics of the problem - in other words, what might be achieved and how.

The launderette campaign is an action group set up to press for a particular aim. We have already looked at how action groups or pressure groups work and seen that they lead an uncertain existence, may not involve many people, and don't need so much formal organisation as permanent committees or working parties. In some cases, it might be best if the action group was nominally independent of the association. It would then be able to get involved in conflicts, without causing trouble for the whole association, but could still draw on the information and useful contacts which the association should possess. On the other hand, it would be difficult for the association to control the action group's activities if there were a serious difference of opinion between the two.

All these sub-groups could be brought together in various ways. Broadly speaking, the wider the range of sub-groups the looser the central committee needs to be. There are five levels at which the central committee could work, ranging from tight overall control to being no more than the servant of the sub-groups.

Executive Committee

The first level is to have an executive committee, which controls all the activities of the sub-groups. This is only applicable when there is basic conflict between the sub-groups and when the association is only pursuing a limited range of aims. An executive committee needs to be especially well organised, democratically elected within the association, and can probably only work well when most of the association's members know and trust one another.

Co-ordinating Committee

One rung down the ladder is the co-ordinating committee, which is useful when the association wants to ensure that all the sub-groups are pulling in more or less the same direction and communicating with one another. Day-to-day decisions are left to the sub-groups. A co-ordinating committee allows for a certain amount of differences of aims and approaches between sub-groups.

Federation

A federation is a group consisting of delegates from all the sub-groups, who come together to exchange information and options, and to give political support to one another where necessary. Federations are more commonly found on a city-wide level, where local groups such as tenants associations with similar aims need to be sure they are not simply being played off one against the other. They are less useful within neighbourhoods. Federations do not exercise any control over their member groups.

Forum

If the sub-groups only need to meet together for the purpose of exchanging information and ideas, the central committee would probably be simply a forum for discussions. This is self-explanatory, but in practice there are few situations where all the sub-groups need to do is talk to one another.

Central Committee

There are some practical jobs which are best done centrally. If every sub-group was putting out a newsletter, for instance, it would be easier and less confusing to bring them all together into one community newspaper. Some secretarial and information-finding jobs could be done centrally, saving time and duplication of effort. A central committee could have the job of a servicing group; rather than running the sub-groups, it would be run by them. Provided the membership of the sub-groups is prepared to take a responsible attitude, this can be a very effective way of doing things.

Community and Neighbourhood Councils

Most neighbourhoods which are organised will have some body which calls itself the Community Association, or Tenants, or Residents Association. But a few places have slightly more ambitious organisations called community councils or neighbourhood councils.

'Community councils' are statutory bodies in Wales and Scotland. That is, they act as a lower level of local government, below district councils, and have certain duties and powers. Usually these are concerned with environmental and other minor matters such as playgrounds. They may also give small grants to local community and voluntary organisations. The councillors are elected in the same way as district and county councillors, but they tend to be less party political. Putting up members for election to such community councils can be a good way for a group to be taken notice of (though it can also upset existing councillors who may not be used to being opposed at an election).

In England, such councils also exist in many rural and a few urban areas but are usually called parish or town councils. Some of the so-called 'community councils' in England are really a form of area participation committee (see 'Participation Schemes' in Part 3). Finally there are some with no official powers or which may consist of delegates from all local community organisations. The Association for Neighbourhood Councils (see Appendix) has information on these organisations and seeks to promote them.

Elected neighbourhood councils are a bit like parish councils in villages - they are sometimes referred to as urban parish councils. As with the local council, their members are councillors elected from among the residents of the neighbourhood. They are thus the most representative kind of community group and are often welcomed by local authorities. But because they spend so much time dealing with the authorities, they need to be careful not to be co-opted, that is treated almost as an extra part of the local authority system rather than as a community group. The other problem, of course, is that organising democratic elections where every adult in the neighbourhood can vote is very time-consuming.

Delegate neighbourhood councils are those made up of representatives of all the organisations in an area: they are easier to organise than elected councils, but apart from that they have the same problems. They can also be out of touch with local feeling, which is less likely with an elected council.

A full discussion of the pros and cons of neighbourhood councils would take far more space than we have here. They should certainly not be lightly dismissed; if neighbourhood groups are to become an effective force for change, then structures something like neighbourhood councils will have to become more and more common. However, groups should also beware of the dangers as well as the opportunities involved in a very close relationship with the authorities.

Part 2

Community Groups and Public Authorities

Introduction

This Part illustrates the settings in which community action is likely to take place and examines the different and often complex organisations which community groups encounter in their efforts to make changes. What issues lead to people getting together in community groups? Is there an element of competition between groups which do form and, if so, can this be avoided? Are there different ways of tackling the same problem? How much do politics come into things? What powers do community groups have? However, before we can consider any of these questions, we need to look at what we mean by the community.

The Community

Often people band together because they have common interests: all that is really meant by a community is such a collection of people with shared interests, and so we hear talk of 'the business community' or the 'West Indian community'. However, most community action takes place in neighbourhoods. To some extent, each neighbourhood is a community - sharing the same shops, schools, pubs etc - but within every neighbourhood there are different communities:

> 'I felt there was more than one community in Southwich. A community is people who meet at a regular place on regular nights at a pub or church or whatever. I think events have proved it - there are maybe a dozen different communities. I felt that one of the sad things was that all the different communities weren't in touch with one another.'

Neighbourhoods vary tremendously, but no matter how well-off they are, there are usually problems of some description. New estates may be badly built and have few of the facilities like shops, pubs or launderettes which other areas take for granted. Bus services and public telephones may be practically non-existent because the powers-that-be assume wrongly that everyone has a car and a phone.

Areas where slum clearance or renovation is going on have the problems of bad housing conditions, rubbish and vandalism.

'The group is mainly owner-occupiers, but the area is split between owner-occupiers and tenants. The tenants are in the worst position.'

There may be different interests, too, between racial groups or generations or between those who have lived in an area for a long time and those who don't lead such settled lives. On council estates, everybody has the same landlord, which is a strong common interest, helpful when forming tenants associations. But estates are often drab and soulless and there tends to be less contact with neighbours than in the older communities.

Blocks of flats create other problems. Lifts and rubbish chutes break down, and because people live on top of one another, noise tends to be a problem. It is also difficult to get to know the neighbours in flats. There are differences between estates, some being seen as desirable and others not. This may lead to friction and jealousy between groups on a city-wide level, rather than groups joining together to tackle common problems.

Geographical differences also have a bearing on communities. In company towns or one-industry areas, such as coalfields, much of a group's time will be taken up with matters concerning that industry: pollution and unemployment. If there is a tradition of high unemployment in an area, more men may be around to experience problems which are usually only noticed by women.

Neighbourhoods vary tremendously

Some areas, often seaside towns, have high numbers of elderly people with special needs. On the other hand, the minorities in such areas may get a raw deal - there may be nothing for children to do. Overspill towns near large cities tend to be very cut-off, with a lot of small children and lonely people. Generally, the distance a neighbourhood is from the town or city centre can have a big effect on community life, as well as on the cost of living.

Community Issues

Many problems within neighbourhoods can lead to community groups being formed. Different issues naturally give rise to different types of groups, but similar concerns may also be tackled in different ways. The quotes in this section indicate some of the variety:

> 'I would like to see the area with less traffic and more play facilities. There's only one youth club for the 10 to 15-year-olds, and there's nowhere for the over-15s to go.'

This shows a concern for safety, the quality of the environment, and facilities for children and teenagers. It would be possible to tackle this problem several ways: by having a big campaign for play streets and a by-pass; a small campaign for a zebra crossing; pressing the council to provide better youth facilities; or organising a youth club or play scheme locally, with or without the council's help.

> 'Every area should have a Tenants Association because people need associations to back them up in their fight for welfare benefits.'

This is concerned with people's need for information and help in claiming their rights. It could lead to: publicity about benefits; putting pressure on Social Security or the Housing Department to be more generous and to provide more information; or setting up a local advice centre.

> 'The area had been pretty good, but once the word got round that it was to be a CPO [Compulsory Purchase Order - for demolition] area, it deteriorated. The streets weren't being kept clean, and we decided that we wanted the area kept clean right up to the very last house being knocked down, and so we organised ourselves to do this.'

This example deals with the familiar process of an area becoming run down after news or rumours that it is to be redeveloped. Tackling this could involve: ensuring that street cleaning and maintenance are not neglected; putting pressure on the authorities about where people are to be rehoused; or fighting slum clearance proposals because people want to stay in the area.

> 'We started the festival because the area was so depressed and we wanted to put a bit of life back into it.'

These people were concerned with livening up an area socially. This could take the form of a community festival, as in this case; campaigning for social facilities like a community centre; running social events such as dances, parties or fetes; or direct work to brighten up the appearance of the area.

> 'I discovered the kids were getting through big gaps in the wooden fence separating the bottom of the estate, near where I live, from the railway. The man from BR came out, we had a row and we threatened to sit on the railway line if something wasn't done. It took a year, but we did get the fencing replaced.'

To some, this might be a trivial issue, but it's important enough if you think your kids are in danger. Sometimes a group getting together over a minor issue will disband after it has succeeded; at other times such small beginnings can lead to the formation of groups with wider aims.

> 'The Tenants Association started off because there was so much feeling about the *Housing Finance Act*.'

This shows the opposite side of the coin - that even important national political issues might be material for community action. The *Housing Act* 1988 was responsible for much community action on council estates. Also the miners' strike led to the formation of many local support groups, some of which have continued in existence as wider community organisations. Groups taking national issues such as this as a starting point often continue by tackling more local issues.

Is your area run-down?

Not all community problems are necessarily dealt with through community action. Certainly in the past, important local concerns such as education, health, employment and consumer affairs have been neglected by groups. However, as groups develop, it seems that many are turning towards broader issues, using the experience they have gained from more specific schemes. There are also wider concerns which affect people as much as, or more than, local issues. Examples include changes taking place in city centres, unemployment in a city or region and rises in public transport fares. Again, these are issues which were not usually associated with community action, but there does appear to be an increasing awareness among groups that joint action in these fields can produce results.

The Council

Almost all community groups have at some time to deal with their local councils. Even for something relatively simple like collecting signatures for a petition, you need to know who to send the petition to and this isn't always obvious. Some groups spend nearly all their time negotiating or arguing with the council. Local councils (and other public authorities) are, therefore, an important part of the setting in which community action takes place and it is vital to know something about how they work.

It is surprising how few people know much about local government, and indeed the set-up is so complicated that it deters all but the keenest. The language used in council documents and correspondence is often baffling. As one person put it:

'I can't understand all the council papers. Council jargon is a load of rubbish to me and I get confused. '

Council language is often baffling

The council system varies from place to place. London has a different system from the rest of England. Wales is more or less the same as England but with some slight differences. Scotland is very different. On top of this, each local authority has quite a lot of freedom about how many departments and committees it has. So all we can do here is sketch the outlines and suggest how you can go about finding out the details of your own local councils for yourselves.

Each local authority consists of two parts. The council is strictly made up of the elected *councillors*, who are supposed to make the decisions. Working for them, and carrying out their decisions, are the *officers*, the so-called 'bureaucrats'. There are also the many thousands of other council employees who actually carry out the services to the public - including teachers, social workers, dustmen and caretakers, to name but a few.

In Scotland local government is divided into regional councils, district councils and islands councils. The different types of council have varying responsibilities and departments. Regional councils cover areas like education, planning, roads, estates and social work. District councils are responsible for such things as environmental health, housing, building, libraries, the arts etc., and there are several district councils in a region. Islands councils are all-encompassing authorities.

The System

Until the spending cuts of the last few years, local government was one of the fastest growing areas in the economy. In many ways, it is run like a big business - not surprising when you consider the value of the property owned by local councils and their large-scale commercial ventures like public transport. As local government grew, it was reorganised into a smaller number of much larger authorities - supposedly to make it more efficient, though many people would doubt this.

'Communication between the two local councils and between them and the county council is negligible,'

said one frustrated community activist.

Councils are involved in business in another way, too. A lot of their income comes from businesses and they are very dependent on the strength of the local economy. They gear their policies towards attracting industry, commerce and investment to the area. One result of this has been the destruction of old city centres and their replacement with office blocks and/or new shopping precincts. Another has been new urban motorway systems.

It is not possible here to give more than a very general idea of how local government is paid for. For one thing, it is an extremely complex subject. For another it tends to change very frequently and guides to it quickly become out of date. The income of local authorities comes from:

- general grants from central government (currently called rate support grant);
- specific grants from central government for particular services or projects;
- income from community charge or poll tax; and
- income from sales and charges (for example sales of land, charges for using swimming baths etc).

Because most council income has come from central government rather than local ratepayers, the government has been able to have a big say in council spending, changing the rules of the game with bewildering frequency. The poll tax system may change this: the intention of it is to create a closer relationship between what people pay to local government and the services they get, although many regard the system as unfair.

Local government is big business

It is also important to distinguish between what councils spend on such things as new leisure centres or improvement schemes (capital spending) and what they spend on staff wages and day-to-day costs such as grass cutting (current spending). Capital spending is mainly paid for from grants, poll tax income and charges.

Although some departments (sometimes called directorates) like social services and education crop up in every area, local councils often differ from place to place in how many other departments and committees they have. There is a committee for each department.

Housing is a good example: in some areas it is a separate department, while in others it is part of a bigger department such as the borough engineers or development department. In a few places it is amalgamated with social services. Often, too, the same department will have different names in different towns; public health is sometimes called environmental health, for instance. Some local authority functions also come under different departments in different towns: community centres might be the responsibility of either education or social services, for example. Youth work may come under education or leisure services.

Recreation is particularly complicated. Every type of local authority has some responsibility for recreation and some divide this into adult recreation and play, and put them into different departments. The department responsible for youth clubs may not be the same as that responsible for playgrounds (on council estates the housing department is sometimes responsible for playgrounds), while playgroups and day nurseries for pre-school children come under social services, and nursery schools come under education. All very confusing for the many community groups trying to get play and recreation facilities.

You will have to find out just how your own local council is organised. An easy place to start is the telephone directory, which lists all the different departments and their subsections. After this, almost all local authorities run an information office or a public relations office, which should be able to answer any questions and provide information such as addresses of councillors and which committees they are on. The library is the other place to go to for information about local authorities. They also keep copies of the Minutes of the council and its committees, which the public can see, as well as facts and figures about such things as how many houses are being built or demolished.

Local councils by law now have to produce publicly available annual reports and provide information on services along with the poll tax bill.

Local authorities don't usually have a proper appeals system for individuals or groups who aren't satisfied with their treatment but there is a local government ombudsman who is not employed by the council and whose job it is to decide on cases where someone feels they have been badly treated by a local authority. The town hall or the library will have the address, as well as information on how to make use of the ombudsman.

Decentralisation

Local government has come to be seen as remote, bureaucratic and not in tune with the interests and wishes of the people it is supposed to serve. A growing number of local authorities have taken note of this kind of criticism. As a result many local authorities are looking for ways to become 'closer to the customer'. One way is to become more open, as we shall see below. Another is to stress consultation and participation (see Part 3).

Decentralisation simply means taking services out of the town hall or civic centre and placing them in the neighbourhoods where people live. It is sometimes, but by no means always, accompanied by forming area

Councils provide services

committees or neighbourhood forums in which local residents can have a say in how their services are provided.

Only a few councils have gone in for full-scale decentralisation where most services are provided on a neighbourhood basis through 'mini town halls'. A much more common version is for individual departments to decentralise their services. Housing has led the way, with a growing number of estate housing offices including a local repairs team and local decisions on letting houses. Other departments which are sometimes decentralised are social services, youth and community, adult education and recreation/leisure/amenities. Outside local government, some police forces have shown an interest in neighbourhood-based policing.

While providing services on a local, easy-to-reach basis is a welcome move, there can be drawbacks. First, while the service is provided locally it is often the case that decisions are still made centrally. Secondly, different councils and departments may have different ideas of what size area a local office should cover. (Some supposedly 'neighbourhood' offices cover populations of up to 50,000.)

Where several different departments in the same council have decentralised in different ways, the results can be more confusing for the customers than if everything were still to be found under one roof in the city centre. Finally, with very few exceptions, decentralisation is a feature of large towns and cities. It has made little impact in rural and semi-rural areas where, because of the cost and lack of public transport, it is arguably even more important.

Councillors

Councillors are elected to represent areas of the town, called 'wards'. Each ward has several thousand residents, though they vary a lot in size. Almost all councillors belong to one of the main political parties (plus nationalists in Wales and Scotland) though there are also Independents and others who represent tenants, ratepayers and other groups. In some rural areas the majority of councillors are Independents.

> 'I'm opposed to the councillor system because they have to toe the party line and can't respond to local wants.'

There is a lot of truth in this. Increasingly, local elections are fought on national political issues, and the concerns of the two biggest parties are often different from the day-to-day things which worry most people.

Another problem with the councillor system is that local councillors, elected to serve the people of a particular ward, have to spend most of their time on specialised committee work, and lose touch with the people who elected them. A recent survey found that most people could not name even one of their own councillors.

Councillors work voluntarily and usually have a full-time job as well as other demands on their time. As local government becomes more complex, they are asked to take on more and more work so it is not surprising that they tend to leave many of the decisions to the officials, especially over matters which aren't of any great 'party political' importance, or where the officials can claim to have expert knowledge of the subject.

Open Government

At the time of local government reorganisation (1974) a lot was said about making councils more open, less secretive. The *Local Government Act* 1972 made it a duty to allow the public into the council and full committee meetings as observers. More recently the *Local Government (Access to Information) Act* 1986 has given councils extra duties to make information available to all local electors, mainly financial information and annual reports. These reforms do not go as far as some campaigners, such as the Community Rights Project, would like. A lot of important decisions are still made in closed sub-committees and in group meetings of the ruling party and simply rubber-stamped at committees where the public is present. By no means all councils are secretive and some have produced very thorough policies of open government. It is worth finding out what your local council's policy is and, if necessary, lobbying to change it. This is one area where the local press and radio are likely to prove powerful allies.

Officials

In most areas, local authorities are among the biggest employers. Their staff range from executives with high salaries to the people who carry out the every-day tasks of public service, including many low-paid part-time employees such as school meals staff and home helps. Community groups usually come into contact with two types of officials: senior officers, and the people whose job it is to face the public.

The senior officers run departments or sections of departments, or manage area or district offices. Examples are housing managers, planners, and area social services officers. These people are members of professions and regard themselves as experts in their own fields. Though they are public servants, they often manage to make it look as if they are giving the orders. They do things according to their own rules and procedures, and often confuse the public by using official jargon.

It is not surprising that people are frightened of red tape and officialdom, as one person told us, and that they feel that if they go through official channels they'll get told off. However, some officials can be very helpful to community groups. They understand the problems and do their best, within their powers, to do something about them. Others quite

It's important to educate officials

simply do not have enough contact with local people to be able to understand their problems.

Community groups have an important job to do educating officials about the effects of council policies on people's lives.

'We haven't really changed anything - just got a few people together to talk to officials.'

The person who told us this was being unduly pessimistic. Getting a dialogue going with officials can lead to important changes in the long run.

The junior officials, who deal with the public on a daily basis, hold jobs like counter clerks and rent collectors. A large part of their job consists of following inflexible procedures which sometimes results in them telling people they can't have what they want, or preventing the public from getting to the higher officials. For this, they take a good deal of criticism, and sometimes abuse, because the mistreated public have no-one else to vent their anger on. But the junior officials don't make the rules; they get pressure from both sides. They tend to side with their bosses - naturally, since they don't want to be out of a job - and sometimes see the public as unreasonable.

There needs to be much more understanding between the public and junior officials, and community groups could make a start in this by making links with the local government trade unions: NALGO (National Association of Local Government Officers), NUPE (National Union of Public Employees) and GMB (General and Municipal). Otherwise, a lot of energy can be wasted arguing about the behaviour of one junior official, when the real problem is the way the whole department is run.

Community groups also come into contact with other council employees. One group is what might be called the junior professionals such as teachers, social workers and public health inspectors. These people are rarely involved in the important policy decisions, but they tend to have more freedom in their day-to-day work with the public than the junior officials.

Another group is the people in charge of local buildings - school caretakers, youth leaders, community centre wardens and librarians, for example. Their first concern is usually to protect their buildings from damage, misuse and mess, which is fair enough, but a few act as if the premises were their personal property. Others will bend over backwards to help community groups by waiving fees, opening at times inconvenient to themselves and so forth. It is necessary to demonstrate to them that you are a responsible group, able to stick to arrangements and to keep promises. Hopefully, they too, will live up to these ideals.

Relevant Bodies

Community groups don't deal solely with local authorities. There are other authorities which are not part of the local council, and there are town-wide voluntary organisations and pressure groups which can help with information, resources and support. We can't give a complete list as the situation will vary from place to place, but what follows is a short description of the main bodies community groups might come into contact with.

Government Departments

For the most part, community groups have little direct contact with central government departments but there are exceptions and, since ultimately the government controls a lot of what local authorities and other bodies can do, it is worth knowing which department is which. The following have responsibility in England and Wales, although the Welsh Office in Cardiff is responsible for several programmes.

Department of Social Security/Department of Health

The Department of Social Security (part of what used to be called the DHSS) is responsible for welfare benefits and its local offices are familiar - perhaps only too familiar - to claimants and community groups acting on their behalf.

The other half of the former DHSS is the Department of Health which is responsible for running the National Health Service. This is done through regional and at a lower level, district health authorities, along with a system of local community health councils with consumer representation. Community health councils have little formal power but if they are active and determined they can often exert a strong influence.

Police

Police forces are part of the responsibility of the Home Office and here, too, there are regional police authorities which include representatives of local councils. At a more local level there may be a police community relations or community liaison committee, open to the public and with community representatives. Again, there are big questions to be asked about how much effect these consultative bodies have, and much depends on their attitudes and those of the senior police officers.

Probation and After Care

The Probation and After Care Service is part of another government department - the Home Office. Probation officers work with people who have appeared before either criminal or matrimonial courts and also with prisoners and ex-prisoners, including young people who have been sent to detention centres or borstals. The Probation Service is also responsible for arranging community service by offenders under the *Criminal Justice Act* 1972. Basically this is a scheme whereby people, who could have been sent to prison, agree to do unpaid work, usually at the weekends, for their community instead. Although part of the system of law enforcement, the service is a social work agency and some officers become involved with community projects.

Department of the Environment

The Department of the Environment is the government department dealing with housing, planning and transport. It has regional offices which can sometimes help with information and expert advice. One of its off-shoots is the Housing Corporation, which gives grants to housing associations and controls their activities. Housing associations are usually voluntary organisations trying to meet housing needs. Some cater for special groups like handicapped people or single parents. Some are based in neighbourhoods and managed by local people, others are staffed by professionals and run by committees. Community groups usually have to deal with, or even form, housing associations if their neighbourhood is in a Housing Action Area where older houses are being improved. Housing associations are also beginning to take over large estates from local councils. Some housing associations, especially in the big cities are becoming very large indeed, having a thousand or more tenants.

The Training Agency

The Training Agency used to be called the Manpower Services Commission (MSC) and has been responsible for the various job creation and training programmes over the years. It now runs two main programmes: the Youth Training Scheme (YTS) and Employment Training (ET) for adults. Since the Community Programme (CP) was scrapped, this has become a less important organisation for community groups than previously, when CP funded a very large number of community projects up and down the country. Community organisations are rarely in a position to provide the thorough on-the-job training that ET requires.

The Scottish Office

The Scottish Office in Edinburgh carries all the functions of government in Scotland. It has more devolved powers than the Welsh Office. The Scottish Office has responsibilities for education, police, fire, law and criminal justice, building, health, property management and social work.

Other Organisations

Councils of Voluntary Service

Most places have town-wide voluntary organisations. These are often

co-ordinated by a Council for Voluntary Service (CVS). The CVS should be able to help with information about other, perhaps more specialised, organisations and about local charitable trusts and other sources of funds. Affiliating to the CVS may give you access to duplicating or photocopying equipment. In most towns there are youth organisations, voluntary organisations for the elderly and councils of churches.

Specialist help can be invaluable

The Trades Council

The Trades Council is composed of representatives from trade unions, though other people with special knowledge (and this may include community groups) can be invited onto its committees. It discusses not only trade union matters but community issues as well, and could often use a lot more information from community groups. In return, it can help organise support for campaigns and demonstrations, and put groups in touch with unions who may be involved in the same issues. Again, community groups can affiliate to the Trades Council.

Pressure Groups

Larger towns and cities usually have a number of pressure groups, which can often help with information, advice and support. One of the best known is the Child Poverty Action Group, dealing with welfare rights and low incomes. Often there's an action group dealing with housing; there are also campaigns against the cuts, campaigns for women's rights and for battered wives, and pressure groups dealing with public transport. Some places also have 'alternative newspapers', which can be a way of getting something into print if you think the local evening paper won't handle it properly. A CVS should have the addresses of organisations like these.

Citizens Advice Bureaux

The place to go for all kinds of personal advice, especially about social services, benefits, and citizens' rights is the Citizens Advice Bureau. Most fair sized towns and cities have them, as well as London Boroughs. Your local CAB should be able to tell you where to get any information or help you want, even if it cannot provide it for you on the spot.

Housing Advice Centres

Depending on where you live you may have a local Housing Advice Centre. If there is one it will probably be run by the local council, and you have the right to advice (and often help) whatever your housing problem. HACs are meant for everyone - home owners as well as tenants. The council will tell you if there is an HAC in your area. Some HACs are run by voluntary organisations, such as Shelter and the Catholic Housing Aid Society.

Community Law Centres

Even more scarce are Community Law Centres. Law centres exist to provide free legal advice and help from solicitors to people who could not otherwise afford it. If you do not know if there is one in your area and you cannot find it in the telephone book, your CAB will tell you if this kind of help is available.

Local Enterprise Agencies

In almost all regions of the country there are now various agencies promoting and supporting community business and local employment projects. These may go under the names of 'Local Enterprise Agency' or something similar, and are a very important source of information, training and possibly funding if your group is trying to create local job opportunities or community businesses. Most of the larger local authorities also have an economic development department or unit which may be concerned with helping grass roots initiatives to get started as well as with the more familiar work of attracting and keeping bigger firms in the area. Some relevant national organisations are listed in the Appendix and these will be able to tell you whether they are active in your area. In general, this kind of work is further advanced in Scotland than in the rest of Britain.

Politics

Community groups are often very wary about politics. Although they may be anxious to keep politics out of things the fact is that all the issues community groups deal with are political, from the welfare of the elderly to job creation or the sale of council estates. Finding any real solution to these problems, rather than just muddling along and making the best of a bad job means getting involved in politics, though not necessarily in party politics.

The trouble is that 'politics' has become a dirty word. To many people it means promising the earth, then delivering yet another economic crisis. It can mean putting the interests of those in control - the bosses, the big trade unions, or the faceless bureaucrats - first and letting the rest go hang. But politics exist outside Westminster and the Town Hall. The very fact that people meet together in groups means that they are in a position to raise issues, discuss them and then act according to their conclusions.

Political action is involved wherever a group tries to further the interests of the people it represents. Political issues are any issues which have anything to do with power and money - in other words, almost all issues. Many community groups are already involved in politics, often without realising it. But when ordinary people say they don't want anything to do with politics and actively avoid it, they are leaving those who are powerful free to continue to carve up the cake their way. You can't take a neutral stand when you talk about community action.

Issues tackled by community groups are rarely isolated ones. They have their roots in bigger national problems. So vandalism may have something to do with youth unemployment; lack of housing repairs may be due to government spending cuts. Community action can easily make the mistake of trying to push back the ripples at the edge of the pond without anything being done about the bricks being thrown into the middle. This does not mean that local groups are ineffective - quite the opposite. People who live with the problems should be the ones to take action, but we do feel that it can be dangerous if community action stops at getting some purely local improvements. Often such improvements can be at the expense of others, equally needy, but less well-organised. Unless community groups make links with one another and with others' action on similar issues, the opposition will continue to play the divide and rule game which has always been one of the most effective political tactics.

Critics of community action sometimes refer to it as parish pump politics - concerned with symptoms but not with what causes the problems. They see community action as a bit like someone sweeping up an endless stream of rubbish blowing into their back yard, without ever looking outside into the street to investigate where the rubbish is coming from!

People naturally feel most strongly about their own areas. A member of a community association on a council estate said:

'It's the old saying: "Out of sight, out of mind." I don't care for people on the other estates because here I can see all the suffering going on. Just as I'd feed my own kids before next door's I feel the same about the estates.'

Others emphasised the importance of local groups, which were more in touch with people than city-wide organisations:

'When you start expanding like the Tenants Federation, you lose track of the individual tenants, who are what it's all about. The grass roots come first.'

Finally there's the problem of time. Most groups are over-stretched just trying to meet local needs and tend to see wider concerns as something to be tackled once they've got on top of their local work:

'I wouldn't honestly say there was rivalry between groups. I would think it's primarily that people get too concerned with their own little patch, their community. Anything outside they feel is not really their concern. Just the problems in their own area take too much time.'

All these views may well be quite reasonable and valid but just as co-operation is better than competition within a community, so is co-operation between communities important. If this doesn't exist, there is a very real danger that groups who only try to effect change on a purely local level may inadvertently gain something at the expense of another equally needy but less well-organised area. Lack of communication and co-operation can leave the door wide open for the authorities to use divide and rule tactics.

Community Groups and Power

A lot of people are very aware that even the strongest community groups have got big odds to fight against:

'Some people enjoy being David against Goliath: I think that as a small group we can challenge the giants.'

However, in order to be effective, community groups need to be realistic about their own power and the power of whoever they're tackling. Also they need to understand what makes some people and organisations powerful and others not.

One factor is economic power and community groups should never forget that business and trades unions can often be as powerful in local politics as they can in national issues. Community groups can discover that what they think is a conflict with a council is, in fact, a conflict with business interests. It is also important to remember that a small group is only likely to make an impression on a big organisation, like a local authority, if it acts together with other groups - or at least is aware of what others have done. As one person pointed out, even if you lose a battle with the council, you can ruffle their feathers and make a way for someone else to win.

There are five main ways in which local councils and other authorities hold power over community groups. The first, and perhaps the most obvious, is their control of resources. They have the money and they decide where it should go, according to their view of the public interest. They can certainly be influenced by community groups, but remember that they are also influenced by business interests and by residents in the better-off areas, who themselves have more power than working-class groups.

Authorities also hold power because in most cases they control the timetables; they decide not only what shall be done but when. Using delaying tactics is one way of overcoming local opposition, or taking the steam out of a campaign. Even when this is not done deliberately, the time it takes for matters to pass along the bureaucratic conveyor-belt can demoralise all but the most committed groups.

Thirdly, power comes from having expert knowledge or from convincing others that you have. Few people will argue with an expert. One

woman said that to approach the council takes a lot of guts and not everyone can stand up to them, and this is particularly true when you're dealing with experts. However, experts don't always agree among themselves - often you can find your own expert advice, which conflicts with what the officials are saying. Above all, people who have to live with bad housing, transport etc are in their own way experts on the subject and that should not be forgotten.

The least obvious, but perhaps the most important, way in which authorities exercise their power is by defining the problem. In nearly

Few people will argue with an expert

all cases they will tell you what will be pre-conditions for meetings, such as that no individual complaints are to be raised, thus putting the discussion on their terms. You may end up using their jargon, seeing their reasonable point of view and finally believing that people in your area are being irresponsible and asking for too much.

Last of all, there is a saying that information is power and it is true that having information at one's fingertips and knowing useful people is helpful. Usually the authority will have more information on the subject under discussion than a group will, but this is not always so. Quite often a community group can show that the authority simply hasn't done its homework. This is the main area where a well-organised group can begin to compete on equal terms with the opposition.

Yet community groups are potentially powerful in specialised ways, if only they can realise it. They can combat the powers at the disposal of their opponents in various ways. Good use can be made of publicity, for example shaming people into doing what you want of them. Special local knowledge, which is rarely available to local councils, can be put to good effect. In some cases, councillors can be shown that they will lose votes if they ignore local needs. If necessary, direct action can be taken - demonstrations, strikes, sit-ins and boycotts do get results. In other respects, the dice are well and truly loaded but knowing how the game is rigged is the first step towards deciding your tactics and getting to grips with the tasks in hand.

Links With Other Community Groups

In order to get beyond the local neighbourhood, community groups need to make links with other bodies. Most of all, they need to make links with each other.

The immediate value of meeting other groups is in swapping information, experiences and ideas. A tenants association member said that she enjoyed meetings between community groups:

'because you get to hear different points of view - though we're all on the same course - and I'm learning from them as they are learning from us. I want to learn so that I can pass my knowledge to other areas, so they can start associations too.'

Another person said:

'Seeing what other people in other groups could do for themselves made us think that we could do things in our area.'

Every group can learn from the experience of groups in other areas working on the same problems. A volunteer in an advice centre said:

'We visited other centres sometimes and one group came to see us once. I thought those meetings were very good. You got other people's points of view and could get information and advice from them to use in your own centre.'

Joining forces can also give more weight to your cause:

'Groups with similar aims should get together - it's a question of quantity not quality sometimes and the more people are seen to get involved, the more you get done.'

Although people readily agreed that such links were useful, few groups had made a regular habit of meeting. This can be frustrating:

'There's no unity, although the potential is here. We need co-ordination for a united front on the housing problem but people only seem interested in their own immediate neighbourhood.'

As one woman put it:

'There's got to be a fairly threatening or pressing issue to bring groups together.'

She had experience of just such an issue, when an increase in heavy traffic through a town brought several local groups together to fight the threat. Without such a pressing issue, it seems groups are not prepared to give priority to meeting up with others. Immediate local needs may be more urgent and are certainly more obvious. However, there are long-term as well as short-term considerations and to be effective in the long term often means being less effective in the short term. Time spent now on picking the brains of other groups should repay itself handsomely in the future; another group may well have tried the approach you were considering and found that another way was better.

Apart from irregular meetings between groups involved in similar action, local groups sometimes need to make formal links with one another. In many towns there are federations of groups with similar aims - council tenants associations or groups sponsoring playschemes, for instance. In a federation, each member group is free to pursue its own course of action but there is room for a regular exchange of information and experiences and the possibility of joint action over city-wide issues:

'It was obvious that we need to work together, otherwise we would be working against each other, so the Federation of Traffic Groups was formed.'

Similarly, the whole federation can add weight to a member group fighting a local issue. One of the problems of federations has been mentioned: they sometimes lose touch with the people they're representing. Another danger is that the people who get elected to represent the group on a federation may be more interested in the status it will bring than in representing the group. Or they may simply get so sucked into the bigger issues that they have no time to be involved in the activities of their local group.

Federations can only survive if they are based on thriving, grass-roots groups; their strength and their actions must derive from the work of the individual groups. It follows that there must be room in federation meetings to discuss local problems, as well as the bigger issues - and to see how the two fit together. It also means that a group's representative on the federation must be someone who is actively involved in the group's local work. If possible send two representatives: one regular one, and vary the second to give every member a chance to become involved in things outside your own patch.

Finally, there are also issues which, while they affect everyone daily, are too big for a local group to tackle on its own:

> 'Bus services, fuel costs and expenditure cuts affect everybody and by getting involved in these things we are helping people in a wider area. Its just that things like local dereliction seem to be more immediate. We need to make everyone aware of the shortcomings of the system and of the need to stick together and fight it.'

Really effective action over bigger issues such as these will probably need to involve organisations other than community groups but, by joining forces, community groups can at least start the ball rolling and insist that those in a position of greater power, such as trade unions, see the problem and take action.

City-Wide Organisations

In many areas there are groups campaigning for improvements in housing, transport, and more pre-school provision, to stop cuts in public spending and so on. These groups are usually composed mostly of professional people and students, but often want to involve local community groups as well.

Local pressure groups often have valuable information about the city or region. They may also be able to take up issues which go beyond one particular neighbourhood. If, for example, a neighbourhood advice centre came across some form of discrimination against women, there might well be a city-wide group dealing with women's rights, which could take up this issue more effectively.

It is worthwhile, then, keeping in touch with such groups, but the comments of some of the people we interviewed suggest that there is little to be gained from going further and actually joining them. One woman who had attended a meeting of a regional housing action group said:

> 'They were all community workers and people with higher intelligence and there were no residents there. I left school at 14 and wasn't interested in anything there except sport, so I feel inadequate at those kinds of meetings. If I came out with something it would sound ridiculous.'

It is true that such groups are usually composed of more highly educated (though not necessarily more intelligent!) middle-class people, who may use different phrases and have different ways of doing things from community groups. There are exceptions, but most community activists attending meetings of middle-class pressure groups will probably feel much the same as the woman just quoted.

A city-wide organisation

Another kind of city-wide organisation, more directly relevant to community groups, is the resource centre. Resource centres were set up to provide services to local groups - from printing equipment to expert advice - and to offer a central place where different community groups can meet together. By no means all cities have one, but where they do exist they are very useful. Resource centres usually have enough funds to pay staff, as well as provide free or low-cost services. They are often managed by committees including representatives of community groups.

Finally, there are more specialised resources, such as law centres or some housing advice centres, which may be independent of the authorities and able to help community groups in their particular fields.

National Organisations

A wide variety of national organisations deal with community groups. In dividing them up into four main types, we run the risk of ignoring the fact that most do not fit exactly into one type or another. There is a lot of overlap and this should be borne in mind. We are unable to deal with even the most important ones individually, but have listed the names and addresses in the Appendix.

The first type are the national pressure groups, some of which (like Shelter, or Age Concern) are well known, others less so. These organisations usually have a London office (often with paid staff) but rely on local and regional groups of volunteers to do much of their work. The local groups are really pressure groups of the kind looked at in the previous section. The central office will usually deal with any specific enquiries, as well as putting you in touch with a local group if there is one. In addition, they produce regular information bulletins and reports. These are often free to groups which pay an annual subscription, while other groups and individuals can buy reports of particular interest to them. The best bet may be to write off for a list of the literature they have produced to see if there is anything which could be useful to you. National pressure groups, like local ones, often want to draw community groups into their work and it's worth making sure that you don't enter into a relationship with them which involves your group being taken over. They may, for instance, try to persuade your group to become their own local pressure group.

There are several national voluntary organisations with local offices. Some, like the Citizens Advice Bureaux, are there to help individuals; others, like the Community Development Foundation run local projects; many of these organise conferences, which might be of interest to community activists.

The third type of national organisation exists to service community groups, sometimes employing staff in local areas to do this. An example is the Pre-School Playgroups Association, which helps groups trying to set up provision for the under-fives. There are also organisations providing free advice to community groups on legal matters, public health (which includes a lot of housing problems), welfare rights and many other subjects. There is no great problem with using these organisations, except perhaps that many of them are run on a shoestring, are overworked, and may expect something in return for their help, such as a small donation or an offer to sell copies of their newsletter locally.

Just as community groups with similar aims often band together in a city to form federations, there are a few national federations of community groups, such as the National Tenants Organisation, or the

Association for Neighbourhood Councils. If your group seems to fit into one of these federations, it's a good idea first to obtain some of the national federation's literature to get some idea of what its views are. Occasionally there are rival federations and a few may hold strongly to political beliefs which your group may or may not share. It is clearly important, if community action is to become more than just a local phenomenon, that community groups should join forces nationally: national federations are very valuable. As few of them, if any, have much money, and because they are federations, in which each member group should play a part, it is reasonable to expect that if your group joins one you may from time to time have to take on part of the federation's work, for example helping to produce a newsletter.

Trade Unions

Community action and the trade union movement spring from the same roots - the desire of ordinary people to get a fairer deal from those in power and to have a say in what goes on at work and in the community. Of course there are important differences too. Trade unions have a

Poor people often get hit the hardest

much longer history and are much bigger and more organised. They also have more power - there is no real equivalent in the community to the ability to go on strike.

Occasionally, the interests of community groups and trade unions may conflict: a new factory may bring both increased employment and environmental problems, for example. However, usually the well-being of a community is closely tied in with local job opportunities and wages. The past few years of cuts in public spending have greatly increased the need for community groups and trade unions to get together. Cuts mean higher unemployment and poorer services to the community - and it's the lower paid workers and the poorest communities which get hit hardest.

The local Trades Council is a useful starting point for community groups who want the support of trade unionists. The Trades Council is a body of trade union representatives from several unions covering a town or city, rather than an industry. It works on community issues as well as industrial ones and often co-opts other people (including community activists) onto committees dealing with community problems. Even if you don't want to become so involved with the Trades Council, they will probably support your cause if they think it is a good one, by making public statements or even by helping with demonstrations.

Local branches of individual unions are rather different from their national leadership, about whom we hear so much. It is best to forget any views you may have formed about trade unions from the press and approach local branches with an open mind. The unions most relevant to community groups are those of public employees: the National and Local government Officers Association (NALGO), the National Union of Public Employees (NUPE) and the General and Municipal (GMB). Roughly speaking, NALGO members are in the local government professions, while NUPE members tend to be in the lower paid jobs. A lot of GMB members do the lower paid jobs in the Health Service, and another relevant union here is the Confederation of Health Service Employees (COHSE). The Transport and General Workers Union (TGWU) is also relevant, especially over public transport services. The Union of Construction and Allied Trades and Technicians (UCATT) branches have been very involved in housing policy.

A further point in favour of co-operation between community groups and trade unions is that they can learn something from each other. Community groups could draw on the vast experience of tactics and organisation possessed by the trade union movement, while many trade unions ought to become more aware of the kinds of issues raised by community groups and the relationship between industry and the environment.

Part 3

Taking Action

Introduction

Before a community group takes action over any issues, various points need to be taken into consideration. Are you going to involve yourselves in the task of setting up a project, like running a playgroup, or are you trying to obtain something from the authorities, which will call for pressure group action? If a task group is formed, have you thought about the sort of people you need, how to get financial support and obtain a base from which to work? If a pressure group is formed, to what extent do you see yourselves becoming involved in conflict or co-operation with the authorities?

No one can suggest a set formula of tactics to be used in a given situation. This is because groups differ in such things as size, strength, the length of time they have been established, what they are trying to achieve and the local political situation.

What we have done is to look closely at possible ways of organising campaigns and to give examples showing how some groups have made use of different tactics successfully. We have also looked at the importance of keeping a flow of information going between the group and the community it serves, outlining various ways of receiving and giving information. We have then included a section on using the media in order to reach a wider audience than that reached through more neighbourhood-based publicity. Finally we have discussed the different sorts of people who, because of their particular skills and experience, may be useful to community groups.

Ideas Behind Community Action

There are three main ideas behind the development of community action which we want to look at here: these are direct action, self help and participation.

Direct Action

The main beliefs behind direct action are: that the proper channels do not work very well as most MPs and councillors are too remote from the

people they are supposed to represent; officials have too much power;
people are dealt with as numbers or cases; burning issues are turned into technical or financial problems; and party politics are often remote from everyday life.

> 'We felt that democracy wasn't working. Decisions were made in the Civic Centre, which didn't represent the local people.'

This comment illustrates well why people become frustrated by the system and want to take things into their own hands. Another person said:

Direct action

> 'People can be very strongly politically motivated but so disillusioned by what they see that they either say there's nothing we can do or it's all corrupt. So they become critics like I was, unless someone throws a spanner in the works and asks what are we doing? Many people just grumble or complain among themselves but do nothing.'

Direct action aims to combat this apathy. In response to the shortcomings in the system, which we have already outlined, some people have begun to take things into their own hands. Squatters are a good example: hundred of families are homeless while perfectly good houses are standing empty, but delays and bureaucratic rules make the obvious solution impossible, unless people take action for themselves.

Self Help

The point of self help is basically to get people to look after themselves. A lot of people are bad managers, a lot of them are frightened of red tape and community action can help to reduce this. The idea of self help is that it is better to help oneself than to be helped. However, there are some knotty problems behind this simple statement. Why is it thought to be so bad to receive help? Perhaps because to receive help is to be seen as a failure and our society is geared towards the winners rather than the losers. Also people receiving help often have to pay a high price for it, not in money, but in being made to feel they are inadequate or second-class citizens, when it's really our society as a whole which is inadequate in its failure to provide opportunities for everyone to live a rewarding and useful life. If groups and communities are to be encouraged to help themselves, why do we also have to pay for services which may be badly run or of the wrong kind?

The people we interviewed had different views about the services offered and we have used attitudes towards one particular department to illustrate the range. Some were suspicious or resentful:

> 'There's distinct advantage in local people doing things for themselves. The Social Services don't deal with people in the same way as we do and don't understand the problems and are not trusted like we are. People are even suspicious of the community workers, but not the local people in the centre. Social workers are all for sticking in the office - they don't visit their old people very often. Sometimes it's days before you can get them out and doctors are just the same. We're more in touch with people.'

Others saw themselves as working side by side with existing services:

> 'The group has contact with Social Services - we get visits from the home help supervisor and channel some requests to Social Services.'

Others viewed the department even more favourably:

> 'The Advice Centre could do with some qualified people, some social workers who could really help people, not just ring up the Housing Department for them.'

Another vital question is whether self help is encouraged by the authorities, as it takes the place of services which should, in fact, be provided by the State. If one group sets up a parent and toddler club, for example, will this mean a lessening of pre-school provision for the whole area?

> 'Because of the cuts in Social Services, we were asked if we could take over the visiting of all the registered blind persons. As this was beyond the manpower resources of the group, it was decided to circularise all churches in the area with an appeal for volunteers.'

How would your group react to such a request? Again we found that groups varied in their attitudes:

> 'We tried not to do the things the council should have been doing, unlike some groups who give the council what they want - cheap labour.'

The council uses the fact that there has been community action as an excuse to delay municipal action even further.

Perhaps there are no easy answers, but there is a need for very careful thought before embarking on any scheme. One person described the conflict like this:

> 'In a sense there's a bit of a contradiction because on the one hand, community development is trying to get people to stand on their own feet - to help themselves to do things in as many ways as possible, and on the other hand, it's helping them to stand on their own feet to get their rights to depend on the State, so it's one step forward and one back.'

Self help, especially when it is done in co-operation with others in the same boat, helps to take away feelings of being somehow second class.

> 'It's for people like us, run by people like us and the lasses up at the hut are the sort you can talk to.'

Comments like this demonstrate the need for a grass roots approach. However, we must also ask why such feelings exist in the first place and why the welfare state makes such a bad job of helping people. If the authorities really want to see communities beginning to provide their own services, from running playgroups to setting up co-operative enterprises, they should give such communities practical and financial encouragement. One person involved in a warden scheme said of the local Social Services:

> 'They're apt to let us get on with it, but I suppose they've got a lot of work and they're just passing the buck. What we really need is a paid warden helped by volunteers, but they say they've no money.'

Finally, how far should communities go in terms of self help? Are there some issues or problems which communities would not want to tackle? For example, would your group be willing to police the neighbourhood? Or take over the houses from the council and manage them yourselves?

Participation

Many people would agree with the criticisms of local councils set out at the beginning of this Part but would argue that the answer is not direct action or self help but for community groups to get themselves involved with the politicians and bureaucrats and try to change the way they work. Such people would see participation as the main value of community action. In recent years their views have been echoed by a growing number of local authorities, stung by criticisms made by the government and anxious to involve the public to defend local jobs and services.

While participation in local government is not new, it has been boosted recently by moves to decentralise services and set up area committees, and by various priority estate and inner city projects. On the other hand, many voluntary and community groups which provide avenues for participation have suffered or closed because of government cuts in support to local authorities which support community groups. Some of the difficulties community groups face when involving themselves with council participation schemes are covered later under their own heading.

Approaches

Different issues have to be tackled in different ways. For example, a campaign to get a zebra crossing usually needs short, sharp, action with

a lot of people involved and maximum publicity. On the other hand, you can't expect to get quick results if you are campaigning for a community centre and in this case you would need a smaller number of people who would be prepared to make out a detailed case and to lobby councillors and officials, perhaps for several years. If you are setting up a permanent local service, such as an advice centre, you would need to concentrate on such things as fundraising, management and the training of volunteer helpers.

Try a different approach

The methods you use should also depend on the popularity of your cause and the strength of your support. A group fighting for, say, more help for handicapped people will probably find more sympathy than a group demanding a better deal for social security claimants, so each group will need to use different tactics. It's clear that approaches can vary as much as the different issues groups tackle. For this reason, it may be helpful to begin by dividing groups into two categories which we will call task groups and pressure groups. By task groups we mean those which actually run things themselves: playgroups, community festivals, advice centres, outings and so on. By pressure groups we mean those which ask the authorities either to do something for their area (for example provide employment, repair the houses) or not to do something (for example knock down the houses or start a scrapyard). Some groups are involved in both task and pressure group activities, and there is nothing wrong with this provided it is understood that each side of the group's work needs a different kind of organisation, and possibly different kinds of people.

Task Groups

Very often, one of the main needs of a group undertaking a practical task is a large active membership. One Secretary of a community festival committee explained it like this:

> 'With the Festival, you have to have participation from the residents. You can't have a big carnival parade if no one wants to turn out or build floats.'

A festival is a particularly big undertaking, but even a playgroup or a bonfire night requires plenty of helpers, if all the work is to be done properly.

Members' Responsibilities

Although it's important to have plenty of members, it's even more important that the members you have should be reliable. Everyone is a link in the chain, and if one link fails the whole project might be in trouble. There will be times when people have to let the group down - if a family crisis occurs, for example - but being reliable doesn't only mean doing what you said you would; it means telling the group (in advance if possible) when you can't do it. A group which carries out tasks must be efficient, as there are usually deadlines to meet and this means the time available for discussion is strictly limited. It is vital that everyone knows what their job is, and that information is exchanged between group members. A good Chair and Secretary can do much to help here, but not without the active support of the members.

The group itself may be quite small, but may be relying on outside people, either to help out on the day (for example festivals, running a newspaper) or to give back-up support (for example a neighbourhood watch scheme). In such cases, there must be an efficient way of letting people know what is going on and what they are to do. If a large number of people is involved then you will probably need a newsletter to do this; if the number is relatively small you could nominate someone from the group to make sure everyone is kept informed.

Handling money needs a lot of care, not because people can't be trusted but because the slightest suspicion (even over trivial amounts) can cause problems within the group and rumours within the neighbourhood - and take up a great deal of valuable time too. An efficient Treasurer, who keeps accounts clearly and is prepared to let anyone see how the money has been spent (given reasonable advance warning), is essential. However, the group as a whole also has to be responsible about money and must be in a position to defend itself against any accusations that it has wasted funds. In particular, when the funds have been raised from local people, there will be a strong and quite reasonable interest in the neighbourhood in how the money is spent.

Fundraising

Most task groups not only have to handle money but to raise it. Community groups need funds for a wide variety of purposes: to employ staff for running costs of an office (rent, heating etc); for training; for printing and publicity; to pay members' out-of-pocket expenses and so on. Small amounts of money, such as for the costs of running a community newspaper, are best raised through the group's own fundraising efforts in the locality.

Be inventive

Don't just rely on tried and tested methods like jumble sales but where possible combine fundraising either with a social event which brings the community together (like a festival) or an event which also draws attention to the work of the group or to the issues which it is tackling.

However, this section is mainly concerned with obtaining grants for more costly activities. The number of possible sources of money is enormous although that does not mean that obtaining grants is easy. All we can do here is indicate some of the main kinds of organisation which provide grants to community groups and suggest where to go for more detailed information. If there is one golden rule, it is to be clear about what you want the money for and then to choose an appropriate organisation to apply to. The more specific you can be (including having a very clear idea of the costs involved) the more likely you are to succeed.

Central Government

In order to obtain money from government departments it will usually be necessary to go through your local authority or, if appropriate, health authority. Many such grants require the local authority to contribute a proportion of the money. The main source of government money in England is the Inner Area Programme which only applies to certain areas of certain local authorities. If your local authority is on the list (a phone call to anyone you know in the council will tell you), it will have a map of all the neighbourhoods included in the Inner Area Programme, and you can check whether the area your group covers is included. Despite the name, outside London and one or two very large cities, the Inner Area Programme often includes many outlying council estates and mining villages etc. If your local authority is included in the programme, it will probably have an inner area officer or team of officers (probably in either the planning or chief executive's departments), part of whose job it is to advise and help community organisations to make applications. But then your application will have to be considered along with a lot of others and the council will draw up a shortlist to send to the Department of the Environment, which will make the final decision. Several of the council's own pet projects are likely to be on the list.

The Inner Area Programme is increasingly aimed at projects which create employment or economic opportunities, including training, and are asking for capital grants (for example renovating buildings) rather than recurrent grants (for example employing community workers).

The Voluntary Services Unit of the Home Office can give grants direct to voluntary and community organisations but only for work which is of national significance, even if it is carried out locally. There are also various grants for initiatives in such things as health, education, crime prevention and community and race relations. If your group is involved in these or other specialist areas it is best to take advice from a sympathetic professional agency as to whether and how you might obtain government funding.

Local Government

Most local authorities fund community organisations in their areas. Very few have a coherent policy on this, however, and you may have to approach several different departments to find out what is available. The most likely ones are social services, recreation (may also be called leisure, amenities etc) and housing. Unless you live in London or a metropolitan district this will mean approaching both your district council and the county council (regional council in Scotland). Some local authorities employ voluntary organisation liaison officers and some have a community development unit. If yours does these are the first people to got to for advice on what's available. Otherwise try the chief executive's department which is supposed to co-ordinate the whole local authority. Note that Health Authorities are not part of local government, but are a system of their own under the Department of Health, and may need to be approached separately.

Quangos

These are government-funded bodies which, while being closely controlled by the government, are independent in the sense that they are not directly accountable to Parliament but to their own boards of directors or trustees. Several Quangos give grants to local organisations which are active in their areas of interest. Examples are the Arts Council, the Housing Corporation (governing Housing Associations and Tenant Co-operatives) the Development Commission (for work in rural priority areas) the Sports Council, the Training Agency (formerly the MSC) and the Community Relations Executive. Some of these are connected with regional or local bodies such as regional arts associations and community relations councils.

The European Community (EC)

The European Community (the EC) has a number of different funds aimed at combatting poverty and unemployment in Europe. Several of these are targeted at particular regions (for example hill-farming areas, coal and steel areas). The funds they provide tend to be for very big projects and it is unlikely a community organisation could attract such funding directly but if your local authority has obtained a big grant from the EC for work in which your group has an interest, you could try to get a slice of the action from them. EC funding has proved to be a risky business since money is paid very late, so it is better if your local authority is taking the financial risks! However, EC programmes are developing fast in new directions, and some of these do also provide funds to local projects with potentially wider significance.

Trust Funds

There is an enormous number of trust funds, both national and local, which give grants to community groups. The *Directory of Grant-Making Trusts* is an invaluable source of reference for these. You could obtain a copy from your local library; also your local Council for Voluntary Service is like to have one. Many trusts exist for highly specific purposes, others cover a particular field (such as the arts, or the welfare of the elderly), others still have very flexible policies. Some trusts give only to registered charities but many do not require this. The majority of trusts give only very small grants, whilst the biggest are inundated with applications. However, they are often keen to spread their resources better and to reach less favoured groups.

Businesses

Most companies, except the really large ones, give out only fairly small amounts of money. The best contact locally is likely to be the Chamber of Commerce (or Trade) but again a Council for Voluntary Service may be able to give good advice. If there is a major employer in your area they may have a member of staff dealing entirely with providing grants. The Directory of Social Change publishes material on company giving, and the government is encouraging more such donations. This is a developing area - CDF's booklet *Signposts to Community Action: A Guide for Business* can be useful in urging companies to contribute.

Television and Radio

Following the success of Live Aid and other appeals, television companies are increasingly interested in using the power of the media to attract public donations for good causes such as the Telethons and the annual Children in Need appeal; on a smaller scale the same may apply to your local radio stations. Contact them for information on when to apply, which may only be on an annual basis.

Charitable Status

If your group is catering for local needs, as opposed to being a pressure group or representative organisation, it may well be worth the trouble and the time required to register as a charity with the Charity Commission. This will require you to adopt a suitable constitution and to be scrupulous about finances and may not be worthwhile unless your group is fairly well established and has a lot of professional support.

Advice can be obtained locally from your Council for Voluntary Service (CVS) in England, and also the Scottish Council for Voluntary Organisations (SCVO) and the Wales Council for Voluntary Action (WCVA). Help is also obtainable from national organisations such as the National Federation of Community Organisations (NFCO). You may also need legal advice.

Summary

This has been a short sketch of fundraising possibilities and it is worth remembering that many more detailed guides have been written in this area. Some of the more useful national organisations to approach for advice on fundraising included the National Council for Voluntary Organisations (NCVO), the Scottish and Welsh bodies (as in the preceding paragraph), the Charities Aid Foundation and the NFCO in whichever field of work your groups is concerned with. Locally, the most important source of help is likely to be the Council for Voluntary Service, while in some areas there is a local or regional body such as a Charities Information Bureau specialising in helping groups to raise money.

Being an Employer

Sometimes a community group will be in the position of employing one or more staff (for example playleaders on holiday schemes), or more permanently (for example the warden of a community centre). Some groups employ their own community workers and a few operate a whole service, a good example being tenant co-operatives who may employ housing managers, repairs teams and so on. Employing staff, like managing buildings, can be a mixed blessing for a small group whose members are giving their time voluntarily. It is very time-consuming and can end by taking up all the energies of the group, leaving nothing for other activities.

While the principle of community groups controlling staff is a good one, it is a mistake to look on your workers simply as a resource to the group. They need to be looked after, and they have rights as employees. Unfortunately there are many stories of troubles between community groups and their staff. Some of the main problems are: staff are often inexperienced and poorly paid; staff are often on short-term contracts (for example one year); budgets fail to include proper training and support; and the employing groups do not receive training in how to manage staff.

There is a growing recognition of these problems, however. Some local authorities are realising that it is not enough to second staff to community groups and leave them to get on with it, and may provide some management support and training, both for the workers and the employers. In England, Scotland and Wales the Management Unit of the NCVO (based in London) is a good source of advice and will put you on to any other local organisations which could provide such support for your group and your staff. This is also an area in which CDF might be able to help.

Using Premises

The other problem area for groups running projects is premises. Some groups have their own premises, in which they can do more or less as they like, within the law and the terms of their lease. Others have to use buildings such as schools, church halls and libraries, which belong to other people. Caretakers and managers of buildings often behave as though they own, rather than run, the places. However, they see things from a different angle. The buildings for which they are responsible are valuable assets and your group is only one of several users they have to consider. Often, the shortage of community buildings in an area means that a place is used for conflicting purposes; old people don't usually like to turn up for their lunch club just as the playgroup is thinking about clearing up its chaotic mess!

To avoid conflict, it's worth trying to get a building which suits your needs if that is possible - and unfortunately it often isn't. When you are the newcomers, remember that groups already using the building may consider that their rights are more important than yours. Get to know the caretaker or manager and get to know the other people who use the premises. A lot of difficulties might be sorted out without a fight if people already know one another. Also be careful not to give others cause for complaint against your group.

Pressure Groups

A different set of problems crops up when a group sets out to obtain changes from the authorities. The great advantage of groups doing task-oriented work is that, to a large extent, they control their own work: their work may be hard, but it is fairly regular and predictable, provided they can raise the necessary funds. Pressure groups live a much more uncertain life: they have to be able to respond quickly to the actions or statements of the authorities, but equally they somehow have to cope with long periods when nothing much is happening. They have to know when to compromise and when to keep on fighting, or even when to admit defeat. This in turn means they have to know what people want, and how strongly they want it.

Responding to pressure

A pressure group doesn't need as many members as a task group. Sometimes two or three people can achieve quite big changes, though an efficient Secretary is important if you want the authorities to take you seriously. However, a small, non-elected group is always open to the charge that it doesn't really represent people. So area pressure groups must always be careful to communicate with the neighbourhood. People must be told what is being done and given the chance to change things (especially through public meetings) whenever something important happens.

Newsletters and petitions are also useful for finding out what people want and how much support a group has. All this is quite a lot of work if the group is really small. Although the members of pressure groups may not need to give up as much time on a regular basis as members of task groups, they must be prepared for short bursts of intense activity. For instance, the area might have to be leafleted and a public meeting arranged at short notice.

Often pressure groups have to be able to get to grips with technical subjects (like damp in houses). This involves the ability to check facts produced by the authorities and then obtain facts to support your own case. Members must be prepared to spend time in the library, and, even more useful, to make contacts with other groups acting on the same issues to learn from their experience.

Conflict and Co-operation

Conflict and co-operation are alternative ways of tackling community problems. Conflict involves groups in battles with authority and can include demonstrations, disruption, legal action, publicity campaigns, rent or rate strikes and general non-co-operation. Co-operation involves groups in trying to work through more formal channels and may include lobbying councillors, working on liaison committees and participation schemes.

They are assumed to be totally different ways of working - poles apart - but, in fact, the same group may need to use both conflict and co-operation over the same issue. Many of the examples which follow highlight this combination of approaches at different stages of action. Before the council (we use council throughout this section as the main but by no means the only example of an authority body with which community groups have to deal) will allow any great degree of co-operation, they need to know the group they are dealing with, and be able to take it seriously, so they can be sure their time will not be wasted. This can pose problems for newly-formed groups, who haven't yet had a chance to make themselves known to the council, and who usually have pressing needs which have brought them together in the first place.

Many groups start as protest groups. New groups need to make the council sit up and take notice. This can be done in a variety of ways, some of which involve co-operation - presenting well-documented reports and attempting to arrange for a delegation to meet the relevant committee. The council may well give in to demands straight away, without a fight, in the hope of buying off the group and the group may then feel that co-operation will always achieve their aims. On the other hand, they might need to create a stink before the council are even willing to acknowledge the fact that they exist. One way of gaining credibility is to link with a well-established and respected organisation, particularly if your group can still retain its independence of action. It's useful to be associated with the Community Association (CA). For instance, your Federation is seen by the council as a

Conflict ...

pressure group; the CA, however, is seen in a different light and has more credibility. Even having a name and notepaper can help:

'The Claimants Union was particularly good at getting people grants from the SS [Social Security] and in doing appeals. When someone sent in an application on CU notepaper they always got what they wanted, but when they applied without our help they were done by the SS.'

Perhaps the best way of gaining the recognition of officials is to be seen to be well organised. The results of not being well organised are clearly shown in the following account by a group member:

'I went to a Community Association meeting about housing. The Corporation had asked us what our priorities were for repairs. It was a farce, a shambles. It was very poorly organised and publicised. It was a nice gesture from the Corporation to say we could put our ideas forward - it gave us a foothold. But when the opportunity was wasted it did a lot of damage as the Corporation thought that people weren't interested. And it was also bad because some new tenants turned up, but when they saw what a farce it was they were put off coming again.'

The moral here is that it may be better to have no public meeting than to have a bad one! In some cases conflict is inevitable. If a group sets out to oppose the council's plans for an area, it is very unlikely that the council will be quietly persuaded to change its mind. By the time plans and policies are made public, a lot of work has gone into them, and the people who have put in the work have a strong vested interest in not changing things. There may also be business interests involved, pushing the council in the opposite direction from that which the community wants.

The authorities, and often community groups themselves, frequently think in black-and-white terms of some groups who are renowned for using conflict tactics, and of others who always appear to co-operate. In reality, groups need to be prepared to use both tactics to get the best results. An element of surprise is a useful tactic in itself. Thus, if a group in the habit of using one method, finds this isn't achieving results on a given occasion, they may catch the powers that be off-guard by switching tactics in mid-stream:

> 'The committee doesn't do surprising or daring things, or call the council's bluff any more. It was getting to the point of breaking the wall down between the council and the people, but that's gone now because the council don't respect us because we don't fight now.'

You should not assume that because your cause is worthy everyone will help and co-operate. Sometimes small, seemingly safe issues, like setting up a playgroup, can lead to great conflict.

Here is an example of this and of a group having to use both conflict and co-operation tactics. A Parent and Toddler Group on a council estate had very poor premises in which to meet. The local welfare clinic

... and co-operation

was the only suitable building on the estate and was only used for five hours a week, so the parents decided to approach the Area Health Authority for use of the premises as a pre-school playgroup. During the course of their enquiries, they discovered plans to close down the clinic. They published this fact in the community newspaper. When other residents heard the rumour they also became upset. An OAP who used the chiropody service at the clinic visited her MP, who wrote a letter on her behalf to the Area Health Authority. The reply was encouraging - there were no plans afoot to close the clinic down, and if the situation should change the MP would be informed. Six weeks later closure was recommended. At this, the original group of parents, aided now by

OAPs, embarked on direct action. They gained the support of local councillors and organised a public meeting, at which an Area Health Authority administrator was put in the hot seat. The public meeting was given coverage on local radio and in the local papers. It was suggested at the meeting that a delegation should meet the Area Health Authority to discuss the matter.

Co-operation was being used at this point, and if unsuccessful it was to be changed to stronger conflict tactics, such as some form of demonstration and possibly occupation of the building. The delegation was well received by the Area Health Authority, but the Authority still voted to close down the clinic. The Action Committee found it necessary to resort again to conflict tactics. They aimed at greater press publicity, and organised a day of action where they held activities such as playgroup and keep fit classes on the pavement outside the clinic, to demonstrate what could be happening inside. The Area Health Authority still went ahead with its plans for closure, so the Action Committee eventually occupied the building, which is possibly the ultimate in conflict tactics. They eventually won half their fight - health services were maintained on the estate, but they have not got wider use of the premises.

The group began by co-operating with the authorities by making reasonable requests for use of a building for a right and proper

Be daring, surprise the authorities

cause. They did not have the original intention of causing trouble, or spearheading a campaign against the government health cuts. They had tried persuasion at various stages in their campaign and it was only when they changed tactics that they gained results.

Of course, it must be remembered that militancy only works when you have the power to back it up. Power may take the form of having large numbers of members or supporters to call on. It may be that the group can use influential people such as councillors or it may come from the group's ability to make skilful use of media publicity. Finally, it can come from the group's ability to use threats.

> 'We told the Social Security Manager that if he didn't co-operate with us we'd stand in the dole queue, give out application forms and flood the system. He knew we meant it and so he co-operated.'

The threat of disruptive tactics can be very effective if it is believed. If it is an empty threat, it will only succeed in annoying the opposition and removing the chance of getting anything by friendlier means. Conflict can lead to co-operation, the best kind of co-operation where the council respects the group it is dealing with. Co-operation, if it fails, can lead to conflict, the most useful kind of conflict, because it will be seen by everyone to be justified, since co-operation has proved unsuccessful.

Community groups have very little power. Any dealings with an authority are dealings between unequal partners. It follows that co-operation will always help the council. It may help the group too, but don't be fooled into thinking that because the discussions are carried on in a friendly atmosphere, you are being successful. In the end, results count for more than friendly chats.

Participation Schemes

Participation has been with us for a long time but there are signs that it is coming to be taken more seriously with both central government and local authorities including public participation in many of their new schemes.

The main areas where participation has started to take root are: council housing, especially priority estates; urban renewal and environmental improvement local plans; decentralisation; community social work; community schools and adult education; health education; equal opportunities, especially ethnic minorities and women; crime prevention; and community safety.

Participation can be divided into two main types: permanent participation committees (such as Area Committees, or Equal Opportunities Committees where community representatives form a continuing part of the system); and participation exercises (such as local plans or estate improvement schemes) where the involvement of the community is for a fixed period only). It is not always clear, though, which type you are being invited to become involved with and this is one example of a serious problem with participation schemes - the problem of differing expectations.

Before becoming involved with a participation scheme, it is essential to find out just what is on offer. Is the council simply trying to obtain your views (consultation) or is it offering a real say in decision-making? Is there money available for any improvements to services your group might want to press for? In a participation exercise, how does the council propose to deal with the results (too often they are left to gather dust on some shelf) and will you have a say in that too? In a permanent committee, exactly how will the scheme relate to the other council committees and will it be given any delegated powers including its own budget? We are not suggesting that you should only participate under some conditions and not others (that is your group's decision) but it is vital to know (and to make sure the council knows) what you may be about to get into.

A second problem which dogs participation is the problem of timescales. Participation is often a stop-go affair. It goes when there is an election in the offing or when the government has announced some new funding initiative for community action. It stops when the money dries up or when a report has to go the rounds of endless committees before further progress can be made. So there will be periods of time when nothing is happening, and others when unreasonable pressure may be put on your group to act more quickly than you think is in the community's interests.

Communication and language are another problem. Bureaucrats have their own jargon words which mean little to those in other professions let alone to the public at large. One person told us:

'Their questionnaire was so complex that even the Chair of their own committee couldn't understand it.'

All of this is even more of a problem for those whose first language is not English.

Finally, the way meetings are conducted creates problems. They tend either to be too formal, just like council committees, and community representatives feel baffled by the procedures; or they may be too informal and give the impression that they're just a talking shop which will not lead to action. Finding the middle way is difficult but not impossible; a great deal depends on the Chair (usually a councillor) and whichever officers prepare the Agenda and papers. If councillors are using such meetings to play party politics or boost their own standing, and if officers use them to tie everyone in knots with their own expertise, it is impossible for a community group to play an effective part.

Communicating with the Neighbourhood

The whole point of being a community group is that any action you may take is based on the needs of your particular community. This means knowing what local people want and getting their support. As one resident pointed out:

> 'We can only do what we're doing if we have the backing of local people. Otherwise we'd just be doing what we criticise councillors for.'

Most community groups have only a handful of active members responsible for pressing the demands of the group as a whole. Such representative groups need to get the go ahead from the rest of the community; in other words, they need a mandate. To get this they need to communicate with local residents, and communication involves both feedback (obtaining information) and output (giving out information).

> 'There were lots of times we should have gone back to the residents and asked their opinions but we didn't. I think hardly any of the residents knew about the action committee. Therefore we didn't have the right to make some of the decisions we did.'

This is a good example of a group which clearly had no mandate; information wasn't coming in or going out.

Local Networks

Making use of the local grapevine is an informal way of spreading information and getting feedback by word of mouth. Grapevines can be one of the most useful forms of communication in the neighbourhood. A member of an adventure playground committee said:

> 'The kids have a grapevine and we rarely need to do more than tell one child if we're organising something.'

Some people are well placed for passing on information, or finding out what others want:

A local network

'The Chair of the group runs the corner shop and acts as the neighbourhood listening post. The Minutes are available in shops for people to read.'

There are certain places in every neighbourhood which lend themselves to this, examples being pubs, fish and chip shops, launderettes, the school gate at going home time - in fact, anywhere where groups of people get together and talk. The trouble with grapevines is that most adults don't communicate as freely as the children mentioned in an earlier quote. Information might possibly be passed around between the same circle of friends, without new people being included. There might also be a 'chinese whispers' effect, with information being distorted subtly as it goes the rounds. Most groups have to consider the more formal ways of communicating and keep the local network as a back-up.

Feedback

Feedback concerns finding out people's views, discovering the extent to which a group has support and obtaining ideas and criticisms. There are various ways this can be done. One method is to collect petition signatures, either door-to-door or by standing in a central place such as a shopping arcade. However, a petition is a bit limited. It will tell you how many people agree with your cause, but it will not tell you why they agree, or perhaps more important, why those who didn't sign disagree. There are also other pitfalls in this system. If you stand in a public place you may not reach the people you want to question; for example people in a shopping arcade might work but not live in the area, and you might want residents' opinions. Another approach is the more detailed door-to-door survey. This is more time-consuming but does have the advantage of bringing you into contact with the public, making it possible to have a two-way exchange of views. However, here again there are problems. It is not easy to plan unbiased questions which do not put words into people's mouths. When is the best time to call on people? How many times do you go back when the door hasn't been answered? What do you do if you find that half the people interviewed want one thing and the other half the complete opposite? All in all, surveys need very careful planning and are probably best left for very big, important issues. Some groups now make use of tape recorders or video equipment to get information. They stop people in the street, ask them questions and then play back the tape as evidence to interested bodies.

Public meetings also make a two-way exchange of views possible, as the community group is able to state its case and give a summary of negotiations at the beginning of the meeting and the public can then voice feelings on the matter. However, these meetings are best used to get support for something the group wants to do rather than for finding out what people want.

'We have a mandate to oppose the traffic management scheme and press for the link road to carry the heavy goods vehicle traffic. We were given this mandate at a packed public meeting.'

In this case, the meeting was packed; but there may be times when attendance is very small. The group then has to decide whether this was because the community was not interested in the issue or because there was something wrong in the way the meeting was publicised. Possibly the most useful method of getting feedback from the public is through the community newspaper which we cover more thoroughly in the next section. Such newspapers are usually well read and people see them as belonging to them and their community. In particular, the letters column in a community newspaper is usually extremely lively and people welcome the chance to write their own articles on matters which are giving them cause for concern.

Publicity

A community group must be prepared to use some of its time, to inform the neighbourhood about what is - or is not - going on. This process reminds the public that a group still exists, as well as letting them know about important issues and events. We do not go into great detail about the way community newspapers and posters etc are produced, because this information can be found elsewhere, and there is an address list of useful publications in the Appendix.

Newsletters and Community Newspapers

Newsletters and community newspapers are a widely accepted way of giving out information about a group's activities. Producing a newsletter is a fairly simple task, but running a community newspaper is much more demanding. It has the advantage of being able to give information about several groups, and also gives local residents the chance to air their own views. A great deal of commitment and hard work is needed to get the paper out on time, but most groups we talked to who ran newspapers felt the effort was worthwhile:

> 'I think the Community Association would be struggling if it weren't for the paper. It is a constant source of advertising for the CA and keeps it in people's minds. It also acts as a way of communicating with people without knocking on doors. I did door-knocking before, and it's very time-consuming.'

It was generally felt that people do read community newspapers but one man commented that 'although people read it they don't take it in'.

Producing a newspaper is a large undertaking and to start one requires a great deal of initial ground-work. In some cases, a community worker for example may be able to give the necessary time to help set up such a venture. Newsletters are a quick, relatively cheap way of reaching a wide audience, whereas a newspaper is likely to take up more of people's time (both the producers and those who read it) and will probably be expensive to produce. Therefore, you will need to think carefully before deciding to use either or both.

Posters

Distributing posters is an easy way of getting small amounts of information across to the public. They are also a must if advertising a public meeting, social, or fund-raising event. A well-produced, eye-catching poster is far better than a scruffy thing drawn up at the last minute. Where possible, use local people who are good at drawing - this is one area where students, or possibly teachers in the art department of the local school, could also be very helpful.

Wall Newspapers

A wall newspaper is an interesting compromise between posters and community newspapers. It is a large poster with a lot of information on it laid out like a page of a newspaper.

Leaflets

Leaflets are cheap and easy to produce, although a lot of thought must be put into the content (what they say) and the form (how they look). If the group has access to a typewriter and duplicator, leaflets can be got out very quickly in response to events. They are usually delivered door-to-door, but can also be left in shops, libraries, etc, where people can help themselves.

Video and Photographic Exhibitions

Videos and photographic exhibitions are useful ways of recording an event, such as a carnival or telling the story of a campaign. They can also be used to highlight problems which have a strong visual impact in the community, such as housing and environmental issues. It may be

Videos can look amateurish without an experienced helper

possible to borrow video equipment and make a video yourselves as a group but the result is likely to be amateurish unless you have someone in the group who has some experience. A better bet may be to approach a local body such as a college of further education or a community resource centre, if there is one, which may be interested in making a video for you, to your group's instructions. Some groups, particularly those concerned with giving advice, set up a stall in the local market, which enable them to reach more people than they would in a shop or other building. Other groups organise photographic exhibitions to show the work they are doing, or the conditions they are fighting to improve.

Resources

All the information-giving techniques we have mentioned so far have one thing in common and that is that they require resources in order to produce them. This includes materials (paper, machinery, etc) and people (writers, illustrators, etc). Some areas are lucky enough to have resource centres or print co-operatives, where materials can be obtained and used at minimum cost. However, most do not, so groups need to make contact with as many local institutions and organisations as possible. It doesn't always work but there's no harm in approaching educational establishments and local businesses to get concessionary rates or even free materials. To give some examples, a local printer might produce something cheaply for you in return for some publicity; a local business might have paper stocks it doesn't need any more; or a college, university or perhaps a council might let you use their equipment. There are all sorts of possibilities. We've already mentioned students and art teachers as being helpful if you need drawings, but there may well be a hidden wealth of local talent - you don't have to be a professional artist to be able to draw or a journalist to be able to write. However, many people are shy at first, but the fact that someone has bothered to ask them, coupled with a little bit of encouragement, may well lead to their getting involved.

Use of Buildings

Not all community groups have a building where they are the major users. We sympathise with those who haven't because a lot of time is spent in finding suitable premises, keeping on the right side of managers etc. This makes it all the more important, however, that groups who do have buildings make full and proper use of them.

A building is first and foremost a focal point, a place where activities take place, and where people can come if they want to join your organisation or need help from you. Having a building which is used for certain purposes will create a strong impression locally of what the group does. Not only are buildings useful as advice centres and as places to hold public meetings, they are also useful as a focus for social activities. By running something such as bingo, groups come into contact with people they would not normally see and this is a chance to talk to talk to them, find out their views, and give them useful information. It helps if you display posters on the wall, and have leaflets, pamphlets and books lying around, which people can look at.

Using the Media

The term 'mass media' refers to local and national newspapers, radio and television. Through the media, community groups can reach a much wider audience than they would by using public meetings, leaflets, posters or community newspapers. Media publicity can shock or shame a council into taking notice of a campaign. It is also a good way of spreading campaigns: if people outside your local area know what you are doing, they too might take up the same issue.

There are many ways of using the media. Letter columns in newspapers are perhaps the obvious starting point; letters are particularly good if you are trying to get a debate going, not just make points. They could actually be a better bet than a small article tucked away in a news section but remember that long ones are often edited. To get information or opinions across, put out a Press Release. Discuss the main points with other members of your group, then write it out clearly with the most important facts first. This hits home and captures interest. Put in some quotes, if possible. Don't just approach one paper; draw up a list of all local papers and TV or radio stations which can be contacted.

Think in terms of using the national press for big campaigns. If you can get to know reporters from the local paper or radio station, this will prove useful, especially when you want to say something quickly and be reasonably sure it will not be altered drastically. Local radio stations lay claim to being community based. If they don't come looking for you, why not put ideas for programmes new to them? Phone-in radio programmes are live and, therefore, your contribution can't be edited but you must be very clear beforehand what you want to say.

The same applies to live interviews, but if the interview is recorded you should be able to get the reporter to scrub out anything you didn't mean to say, or didn't put very well. Equally though, they might cut out things you would want to keep in. Remember that a TV story lays great stress on pictures. For example, a local TV station is much more likely to use a story which involves children bathing in the Civic Centre fountains, as a protest against the proposed closure of local swimming baths, than a worthy but dull report on housing. Access programmes, such as Open Door are worth using for long-term campaigns. Here you have the chance to make your own programme, with help from the experts.

What to Watch Out For

The media nearly always have the final say in what they print or broadcast and they can make your message sound sensational or trivial. If you live in an area which has a bad reputation, using the media to point out what's wrong with the neighbourhood often has the undesired effect of making its reputation even worse. To take another example, the media often look for human interest stories, so they might dwell on one person's troubles, rather than making the general criticisms which your group want to put across. Reporters are well practised at putting words into people's mouths and sometimes use planted quotes. Always be very wary of questions beginning: 'Don't you think that...?' If you don't think the reporter is asking the right questions, ask your own and then answer them!

Community groups often complain that editing distorts what they have to say, or that they are not given enough time in broadcasts to say what they want. If you're taking part in a chat show - on TV or radio - and don't think you're getting a fair share of the action, don't be afraid to butt in and make your point. Nobody else will make it for you.

It's also worth asking to see the final draft of anything you have contributed to the press, to check that you haven't been misquoted or misunderstood. They can only refuse and they sometimes agree. The reporter's job is to get a story which will interest the public, is about the right length and doesn't take too much time (after all, he or she will have other people to interview). Your job is to get opinions and facts across to the outside world. These aims are very different, so you cannot expect 100% co-operation from the media. Your best chances lies in having a good idea of exactly what you want to say beforehand; knowing which points are the most important (you may not have time to say everything you want to); and sticking to your guns, even if you are having a rough time. All this means that the group needs to have at least one person sufficiently informed and articulate to deal with the media. It is the problems of a group's publicity representative which we want to look at next.

Representing Your Group

Groups' publicity representatives (their spokesmen or women) need to know their stuff and how to put it across. Self-confidence and a ready good humour are an enormous help and it may be that the strongest character in the group is the best person to deal with the media, even if he or she is not one of the official leaders. There is a danger, though that a group's publicity representative will be adopted by the media, who may then build the person up as the local leader - the media often like to feel they have a local character who can be relied upon to give a down-to-earth viewpoint and who is readily available. This may cause resentment among other members of the group who feel that one person is taking all the credit.

There may also be resentment over money, since radio and TV programmes often pay a fee if a person is interviewed in the studio. As a general rule, anyone obtaining a fee for appearing on behalf of a group should give the money to the group. If you appear as a private individual, that's different, but it may still be worth remembering that you might not have been asked as an individual if you hadn't first become known as a member of your group. The publicity representative may become a regular media personality and lose touch with the group. The risk of this can be reduced by involving other group members where possible and by the group briefing their publicity representative before every appearance. If you're talking to a newspaper reporter, there's no reason why only one person should be interviewed. But if two or more group members talk to the reporter, make sure you are all agreed on what is going to be said, as it looks very bad if group members start arguing amongst themselves during an interview.

TV and radio stations may insist on interviewing only one person for reasons of space and time, but even here another group member can accompany that person and get the chance to see round the place. A group's publicity representative should be careful to credit other people for their ideas, otherwise it appears again that he or she is taking all the praise. Perhaps more important, if the publicity representative makes a point of mentioning the contributions of other people, it shows reporters and the general public that the group is not just the work of one person.

Making Use of People

A small group can sometimes achieve a lot by itself, but usually there are times when it has to call on outside help. There are two kinds of outside help you may need which we will look at separately: expert advice; and political or fundraising support.

Expert Help

Community workers try to help groups develop their own skills where possible. As one member of a housing action committee put it, the feeling of doing something instead of having it done for you is important but there is not always the time for a group to learn to do everything for itself, even if it wants to. Don't be put off by the word 'expert'. We use it here to mean someone with special knowledge of a subject, which doesn't have to come from books; it also comes from experience. So for many purposes the experts may be found in your neighbourhood.

We've already stressed the importance of knowing what local people want and in the process of gaining this information, your group will probably have made contact with many people who could be called in to help. This help could take the form of either giving advice on a specific aspect of the issue you're tackling (for example a local builder who has specialised knowledge on dampness) or adding to the active workforce at a busy time (for example extra help with typing, when a lot of material has to be circulated). However, it is important to make sure that such recruits know exactly what is expected of them and how long they are likely to be involved. Of course, in some cases the expert may end up joining your group more permanently.

Not all expert knowledge the group needs will be found in the neighbourhood, however. An outsider might be needed to check out the facts given by officials or to provide independent evidence which a group could use in support of a campaign. People such as sympathetic architects, solicitors, accountants, planners and public health inspectors come in useful here, though council officers will rarely get involved in a campaign which criticises the council they work for, even if it is another department. Finding sympathetic outside experts can be difficult - it's usually a matter of knowing someone who knows someone. But if your publicity material asks for help, they might contact you.

Another use for outside experts is to use their knowledge to train community groups in dealing with difficult situations. A member of a traffic action group which had to face a public enquiry into a road scheme found this helpful:

> 'We had a mock public examination meeting the other week with an expert and he knocked us down flat in three questions.'

Having had a taste of what line the opposition might take, this group was far better able to cope on the day. However we should issue a word of warning because sometimes outside experts may use their specialised knowledge to their own advantage. If you find that your group is beginning to see an issue from only one viewpoint, it could be because one of your experts is beginning to get you to look at all your problems in terms of their field of experience.

Support

The other way a group can use people is for their influence. They may be people who have the power to sway decisions in the way the group wants or they may have the ear of friends in high places. By lending their support to the group they might increase its credibility or responsibility, or add to its chances of raising funds. Councillors are one such set of people, though some councillors are much more powerful than others. Groups should at least try to gain the respect, if not the support of the councillors for their own area since it is to them that the top officials and more powerful councillors will turn for information about the group. Some group members felt that councillors were not used enough:

'The councillors are aware of the Community Association. We like to think they take notice of it. I think they are wary of it and see it as quite an organisation. I feel that not enough use is made of councillors - people don't realise what councillors can do for them.'

It is clearly worthwhile finding out who are the most important councillors (for example, the Chairs of the main committees) and something of what their views are, as well as keeping in regular contact with at least one of your local councillors. Other influential people community groups can use are local figureheads, such as head teachers, vicars or people who occupy a prominent position in community life. In some areas there will be business people prepared to lend their support to a group and they may well be able to help with fundraising. People like vicars and head teachers may be willing to let groups use their buildings. The advantages are fairly obvious, but there are also disadvantages. If such outsiders are closely involved in the group, they may use their position and their self-confidence to take it over and steer it in directions you may not like.

It is important to try to balance the good they can do against the harm, and if possible to keep such supporters at a distance from the group itself rather than making them full members. If you have a really influential supporter, he or she could be given an honourary position such as President - not involved in the day-to-day work of the group but adding his or her name to letters, appeals for funds etc and making the occasional public appearance. Professional people often become interested in community action and want to help out. Sometimes they are helpful for their expertise, as we have seen; others are more useful for their support, and for who they know. A member of an adventure playground association told us:

'Having professional people like social workers and probation officers on the committee has been a good idea. If it's just local residents we get estate-minded and don't look outside the area. But it also does something for them, too. They can see where the problems originate, rather than waiting until it's too late.'

This sums up the situation well - there are advantages to both sides. But the same applies to professionals as to other outside supporters; their involvement is welcome, but the group belongs to the people in the area and the inclusion of professionals should not change this.

Information and Training

We have already referred to the need for more training for community groups in the section on 'Being an Employer'; the need for good quality information and training is even broader. Luckily, it is a need which is becoming increasingly recognised, though as yet it remains a seriously under-funded area. The authorities now mainly accept that whether a group is running a campaign or providing a service, they will be better if they are trained. By increasing understanding, information and training can reduce unnecessary conflict between community groups and the authorities.

Many of the national organisations listed in the Appendix have an information service to which groups can subscribe, usually at a fairly low rate (CDF itself is one such organisation). Other information sources include local authority community development units, National Council for Voluntary Organisations, Scottish Council for Community and Voluntary Organisations, Wales Council for Voluntary Action, Councils for Voluntary Service and resource centres. Training is required in many areas of community action.

Besides management development, which we have already looked at, there is legal training (for example how to draw up a constitution or a formal agreement with the council or a funding body); technical training (for example a group campaigning about damp will need to know something of the causes and cures); understanding local government etc (some local authorities run evening classes on this); book-keeping and financial skills; how to work effectively as a group or committee combatting racism; and strategies and tactics (for example using the media). These are just examples. Every group will be able to add others which relate to its own special concerns.

Finding people to provide training is easier than finding the money to pay them. For the most part, they have a living to make and cannot work for nothing, though some training organisations may be subsidised to work with community groups. The Federation of Community Work Training Groups may be a good place to start finding out whether there is a regional community work training group covering your area. CDF itself may be able to advise and assist. Locally, a college may be interested in making some of its existing courses more relevant to community groups. Some local authorities extend their training to cover community and voluntary organisations: the social services department might be the best place to start asking but as with so much in local government, the service you are looking for could be located in almost any department.

It is important to include provision for training for yourselves in any budgets you draw up for the purpose of applying for grants. Even hard-pressed local authorities may look favourably on funding or directly providing training for community groups. It is after all, in their own interests to do so.

Changes Large and Small

In this section we ask what sort of changes can occur through community action and look at whether or not they really add up to anything.

Changes in People

We can start with individuals. Community action has certainly changed many of the people who have been involved in it. They have learned things:

'I've met a lot of people from other parts of the city and other parts of the country through the work. It is really interesting and you learn a lot. I have learnt that we shouldn't let power go to our heads. The authorities dominate us and it's important that we should not dominate other people in turn.'

Through taking part, people also become more self-confident and their ideas and outlook on life have changed. Being part of a community is also important:

'It's nice to be stopped in the street to discuss things with people. This feeling of sharing things and feeling a part of something is developing all the time and it makes you feel less alone and isolated.'

The expression used most often by those we spoke to was satisfaction - the knowledge that you are playing a useful part in the community:

'I've gained a lot of personal satisfaction from my involvement. I've particularly enjoyed defeating the system, showing the Borough Council that they've got no right to steamroller things through without taking account of local people's wishes.'

Changes in the Neighbourhood

Most activists also felt that community action had changed their neighbourhood for the better, in small ways, though a few felt nothing had really been achieved.

Community action changes things

'The community groups haven't made any difference to the estate. It's stayed the same. All estates are the same - rough.'

Some had reservations about the extent to which changes would take place:

'People are more willing to look after their own patch, it's rubbed off that far, but there are still not many prepared to help those in the next street.'

Another person noticed how much more lively her estate had become:

'Now people are talking more, people that didn't bother are wanting to do something. Talking in groups, saying what's wrong with the place, whereas before nobody bothered at all.'

Apart from changes of this kind, people talked about having won a variety of things from the authorities, from small play facilities to major housing improvements, and of changing the attitudes of the officials:

'I think the council has become aware that redevelopment is not just a matter of pulling down a few houses and building a few more. They are dealing with people, with communities.'

Wider Levels of Change

On balance, we found that those who have become active in their communities have gained a lot from the experience. There have been plenty of small-scale changes at the local level. Do these add up to anything significant? Some people felt that they did, or at least that they could:

> 'If ordinary people band together and make enough noise, things can change. A lot of minor changes can do a lot more than one major change, I think.'

Others had their reservations:

> 'I have learnt how the council works and how people can change policies at a local level. I'm still very cynical about changing anything at a national level though, and about politicians in general.'

Perhaps it would be over-optimistic to say that community action is already capable of making a lot of small changes add up to bigger ones. Small changes can lead to big changes but not automatically. The problems community activists have to tackle are how to connect the mass of small-scale local action with wider problems and how to link grass-roots groups with bigger organisations without losing their independence and their ability to respond to community need. Small-scale and large-scale changes depend on one another to a large degree. As one person put it:

> 'It's no use community development going on without any other large-scale political change but the large-scale political activity can't be of any use without the community development.'

However, local action can be used as a base for achieving more ambitious change:

> 'I'm not kidding myself that we're doing anything fantastic - we're not changing the world - but it's a start. You think to yourself, "that bloody great brick wall, I can never do that on my own," but once you see someone else is prepared to chip at it, you've got the chance of making a hole in it, even if you can't knock the whole thing down. Unless you bother to find out who else is good at wielding a pick axe, the wall is going to stand for a long time. In other words, groups really do have to communicate with others.'

Women and Community Action

Men dominate most walks of public life. They are encouraged to be more ambitious, while women are often expected to content themselves with looking after the home and family. One result of this is that an area of public life has emerged where women do seem to be more involved than men: community action. As one woman activist put it:

'It's the women who are most involved. They're the ones who can get the jobs done because they're the ones who have to live with the problems. Men can just forget them and go off to work.'

In general it's true that women seem to feel more strongly about community issues, simply because they have to face the difficulties every day. We're not suggesting that men should be excluded from community action, but we do say that women should be encouraged to play as full a part as possible, even if that means some of the men stepping down from their assumed positions of leadership. The experience women gain from community action has begun to influence the male strongholds of the trade unions, local authorities and political parties.

Community action involves women as well as men

Even though women may be keen to become involved in community action, there are all sorts of obstacles in their way. By no means are all put there deliberately by men - many of them result from the assumptions that both men and women make about what things are best done by men and what by women. Take the officers of a committee, for example. In a mixed group, the chances are that the Chair will be taken by a man, but the Secretary may well be a woman, since leading the group is often thought to be a man's job and taking Minutes a woman's. Yet, where there are women Chairing groups, they're just as competent as men - and many men make good Secretaries too. A group dealing with, say, housing is likely to contain more men and be led by a man; a group dealing with the under-fives will probably consist entirely of women. If community groups were to encourage women to become involved in the more political matters like housing, and also to encourage men to take more of an interest in children, welfare, or social events, the results could be very worthwhile. Who knows how much better a playgroup could be run if men were involved in it, or how much more effective a housing action group could be if it were led by women who felt really strongly about the issues involved?

Other obstacles put in the way of women in community action include opposition from partners who don't like the idea of women getting together. One woman described how a women's group was finally forced to fold up because of this and other pressures:

> 'The Women's Action Group collapsed; I don't really know why. Quite a lot of it was political in a way. Quite a lot of the women were brought up to believe that they shouldn't be involved in politics. The Catholic Church stopped a lot of the women coming. Husbands stopped a lot of the women coming - thought they were up to no good, because it was the first time that the women began to think and began to argue points. One or two got jobs because they got the strength from it - that was good. One or two stood up to their husbands - that was good. In the end there were just about three or four of us left who really wanted to go on.'

One conversation we had with three women illustrated the attitude their husbands had towards their involvement:

Annie: 'I don't think if my husband isn't involved, that he can see the benefits to his family. He can only feel the deprivation.'

Betty: 'It would be the same whatever you were involved in. It's because they're men. They don't understand why you can give so much to something.'

Chris: 'He knows if I didn't have this to go to and if I didn't get out I'd take it out on him. It's helped me because if it wasn't there I'd go round the bend. I think if a man's out at work all day, he wants to sit at home with his wife in the evening and moans if she wants to go out.'

Betty: 'They are a bit like children - want you to do what they want. They want you to be there all the time. But I must admit I feel the same if he wants to go out and I don't. Even the most modern men feel, underneath, that the woman's place is in the home at his beck and call.'

Annie: 'I think men are like that because their lives are so full and they don't understand how yours can't be.'

Women tend to work together in different ways from men - not necessarily better or worse. Women in groups often have to follow the men's way of doing things. This is because it's usually the men who have had other committee experience in trade unions or Working Men's Clubs, for instance. It's not just a question of men knowing the ropes and women lacking the necessary experience. It may well be that established methods aren't so effective after all. Perhaps women can contribute fresh ideas. Men and women in mixed groups can learn from one another how to be more effective, but not if the men insist on doing everything their own way.

In any discussion of men and women it's impossible not to make sweeping statements. Many people will feel that what they've just read doesn't fit exactly with their experiences - nor could it, in such a short space. Our main point is that community action is one of the most important ways in which more women may be brought into public life, and that can only do good in the long run. Even so, most women will need encouragement and men will have to be prepared to stand aside sometimes. This can only happen if both men and women in community groups give some thought to the issues we've raised here.

Community Action in a Multi-Racial Area

While a lot of community activity takes place in multi-racial areas, a high proportion of groups working in such areas are composed wholly or mainly of white people. Why do relatively few black or Asian people participate in community action when they face all the problems of their white neighbours and more?

Sometimes the reason is simply direct racism. There are groups which do not want anything to do with black or Asian people. Most community workers and a growing number of local authorities will refuse to support such racist groups. A more widespread reason, though, is the fear of racism, even if that fear turns out to be unjustified in a particular case. Black and Asian people unsure of the reception they will get from a wholly or mainly white group may well decide not to take the risk of turning up to a meeting or offering help.

There is also the problem of unconscious, unintended racism. Many whites who see themselves as non-racist nevertheless make sweeping statements about ethnic groups, based on very little direct knowledge, and treat black and Asian people as though they were to be pitied and helped, not collaborated with and learned from. With some ethnic groups there is a language difficulty. Too few community groups in multi-racial areas put out leaflets and newsletters in locally-spoken minority languages; fewer still have thought about including a translator in their meetings. Apart from deterring those whose English is poor, such attitudes carry a clear racist message: 'you join this group on the terms of the white, English-speaking population' (which may not even be the majority locally). All community groups representing multi-racial areas should take steps to see that they reflect the composition of the area as a whole and are in close contact with all the sub-communities within it. It is not enough to say 'Our meetings are open; people please themselves whether they get involved', unless at the same time the group is dealing with all the things that put Asian and black people off: meetings and written communications being exclusively in English; directly racist comments from individual members; lack of knowledge of other local people's cultures and histories. In most urban areas there are individuals and organisations only too pleased to help community groups in becoming multi-racial and anti-racist (see Appendix) but they first have to want to do so.

Appendix: Contacts

Action with Communities in Rural Areas
Stroud Road
Cirencester
Gloucestershire GL7 6JR
Tel: (0285) 65 3477
Aims to promote any charitable purpose to improve the conditions of life of the people and communities in rural England and Wales.

Action Resource Centre
1st Floor
102 Park Village East
London NW1 3SP
Tel: (071) 383 2200
Aims to apply the skills and resources of business to the benefit of the community.

Age Concern
Astral House
1268 London Rd
London SW16 4EJ
Tel: (081) 679 8000
Promotes the welfare of elderly people and of workers with and for the elderly.

Association of Community Health Councils for England and Wales
30 Drayton Park
London N5 1PB
Tel: (071) 609 8405
Aims to represent the consumer of health services at national level and provide a forum for member community health councils.

Association for Neighbourhood Councils
Room 43, Baskerville Hse
Broad Street
Birmingham B1 2NF
Tel: (021) 200 1027

Aims to advance education in all forms of neighbourhood government.

Association of Researchers into Voluntary Action and Community Involvement (ARVAC)
Unit 29, Wivenhoe Business Centre
Brook Street, Wivenhoe
Essex CO7 9DP
Tel: (0206) 22 4281
Aims to promote, disseminate and discuss research on voluntary organisations, volunteer involvement and community action.

British Association for Local History
Shopwyke Hall
Chichester
West Sussex PO20 6BQ
Tel: (0243) 78 7639
Aims to advance understanding and knowledge of local history.

British Association of Settlements and Social Action Centres
13 Stockwell Road
London SW9 9AU
Tel: (071) 733 7428
Aims to pioneer innovative projects to meet social needs, and provide resources and help for self-help community initiatives.

British Council of Churches
35 Lower Marsh
London SE1 7RL

Tel: (071) 620 4444
Furthers the united action and study of Churches.

Carers National Association
29 Chilworth Mews
London W2 3RG
Tel: (071) 724 7776
Offers advice, support and opportunities for self help to carers of the disabled, the elderly, and those suffering from ill-health.

Catholic Housing Aid Society
189a Old Brompton Road
London SW5 OAR
Tel: (071) 373 4961
Aims to serve the homeless and the poorly housed.

Charities Aid Foundation
48 Pembury Road
Tonbridge
Kent TN9 2JD
Tel: (0732) 77 1333
Promotes and facilitates the distribution and flow of money to charitable purposes by providing covenant services and information.

Child Poverty Action Group
4th Floor
1-5 Bath Street
London EC1V 9PY
Tel: (071) 253 3406
Aims to promote action for the relief directly or indirectly of poverty among children and families with children.

Community Information Project (London Advice Services Alliance)
2nd Floor, Universal House
88-94 Wentworth Street
London E1 7SA
Tel: (071) 377 2798
Offers a range of support services to advice and information workers, mainly in London. Information available nationally, including publications. Coordinates the national network, the Advice Services Alliance.

Community Service Volunteers
237 Pentonville Road
London N1 9NJ
Tel: (071) 278 6601
Involves people in volunteering and community action.

Councils for Voluntary Service (National Association)
26 Bedford Square
London WC1B 3HU
Tel: (071) 636 4066
Promotes, develops and supports Councils for Voluntary Service throughout England.

Directory of Social Change
Radius Works
Back Lane
London NW3 1HL
Tel: (071) 435 8171
Provides training, research and information to voluntary organisations.

Fair Play for Children Association
Westview, Mines Avenue
Aigburth
Liverpool L17 6AL
Tel: (051) 427 0917
Campaigns for children's rights to play, through the provision of more, better and safer play facilities.

Family Service Units
207 Old Marylebone Road
London NW1 5QP
Tel: (071) 402 5175/6
Aims to prevent the breakdown of family and community life by providing services to disadvantaged communities and deprived families.

Feminist Library and Information Centre
5 Westminster Bridge Road
London SE1 7XW
Tel: (071) 928 7789
Provides a library of feminist and women-related books and pamphlets.

Free Form Arts Trust
38 Dalston Lane
London E8 3AZ
Tel: (071) 249 3394
Aims to broaden the influence of arts practice through community work.

Friends of the Earth
26-28 Underwood Street
London N1 7JQ
Tel: (071) 490 1555
Aims to conserve the planet's resources, reduce pollution and improve the quality of life.

Gingerbread
35 Wellington Street
London WC2E 7BN
Tel: (071) 240 0953
Provides day-to-day emotional support, practical help and social activities for lone parents and their children.

Greenpeace
30-31 Islington Green
London N1 8XE
Tel: (071) 354 5100
Protects the environment through peaceful direct action.

Interchange Trust
15 Wilkin Street
London NW5 3NG
Tel: (071) 267 9421
Stimulates community involvement and social action through the use of the arts, media and technical skills.

Joint Council for the Welfare of Immigrants
115 Old Street
London EC1V 9JR
Tel: (071) 251 8706
Advises, informs, helps and represents people with problems caused by immigration and nationality law.

Legal Action Group
242-244 Pentonville Road
London N1 9UN
Tel: (071) 833 2931
Aims to improve legal services to the community, particularly to people living in deprived areas.

MIND National Association for Mental Health
22 Harley Street
London W1N 2ED
Tel: (071) 637 0741
Promotes mental health and helps the mentally disordered. Promotes research in the mental health services.

National Association of Citizens Advice Bureaux
115-123 Pentonville Road
London N1 9LZ

Tel: (071) 833 2181
Provides free, impartial
and confidential advice
and help to anyone on any
subject.

**National Childrens
Bureau**
8 Wakley Street
London EC1V 7QE
Tel: (071) 278 9441
A national interdiscipli-
nary organisation con-
cerned with children's
needs in the family, school
and society.

**National Council for
Civil Liberties (Liberty)**
21 Tabard Street
London SE1 4LA
Tel: (071) 403 3888
Defends and extends civil
liberties within the UK and
ensures the fair administra-
tion of justice.

**National Council for One
Parent Families**
255 Kentish Town Road
London NW5 2LX
Tel: (071) 267 1361
Aims to improve the finan-
cial, legal and social posi-
tion of one- parent families.

**National Council for
Voluntary Organisations**
26 Bedford Square
London WC1B 3HU
Tel: (071) 636 4066
The leading voluntary
agency for the maintenance
and promotion of volun-
tary social action.

**National Federation
of Community
Organisations**
8-9 Upper Street
London N1 OPQ
Tel: (071) 226 0189
Promotes the activities of

community associations
and organisations.

**National Federation of
Housing Associations**
175 Grays Inn Road
London WC1X 8UP
Tel: (071) 278 6571
Promotes housing associa-
tions, and represents their
interests to government,
local authorities, and the
Housing Corporation.
Housing Co-ops.

**National Federation of
Retirement Pensions
Associations**
Melling House
14 St Peter Street
Blackburn
Lancs BB2 2HD
Tel: (0254) 52606
Pressure group campaign-
ing for a better standard of
living for the elderly.

**National Institute of
Adult Continuing
Education**
19b de Montfort Street
Leicester LE1 7GE
Tel: (0533) 55 1451
Advises and consults con-
cerning the interests of
adult education organisa-
tions, institutions and individuals.

**National Tenants and
Residents Federation**
41-42 Estate Buildings
Railway Street
Huddersfield HD1 1JY
Tel: (0484) 43 4943
Aims to protect tenants
rights, and to keep public
housing affordable for the
future.

National Youth Bureau
17-23 Albion Street
Leicester LE1 6GD

Tel: (0533) 47 1200
Acts as a resource centre for
youth work policy-makers
and practitioners in Eng-
land and Wales.

**Neighbourhood Energy
Action**
2-4 Bigg Market
Newcastle upon Tyne
NE1 1UW
Tel: (091) 261 5677
Promotes energy efficiency
initiatives to combat fuel
poverty.

**Pre-School Playgroups
Association**
61-63 Kings Cross Road
London WC1X 9LL
Tel: (071) 833 0991
Aims to encourage the formation of playgroups and
mother and toddler groups
for children under five.

Rights of Women
52-54 Featherstone Street
London EC1Y 8RT
Tel: (071) 251 6577
A pressure group to
achieve legislation which
benefits women and is de-
termined by women.

Runneymede Trust
11 Princelet Street
London E1 6QH
Tel: (071) 375 1496
Provides information on
immigration and race in
Britain and the EEC.

Share Community Ltd
64 Altenburg Gardens
Lavender Hill
Clapham Junction
London SW11 1JL
Tel: (071) 924 2949
Helps disabled people and
promotes them into the
everyday working world

by training, research and information projects.

Shelter, National Campaign for the Homeless Ltd
88 Old Street
London EC1V 9HU
Tel: (071) 253 0202
Campaigns for the provision of decent, secure and affordable housing as a basic human right.

Town and Country Planning Association
17 Carlton House Terrace
London SW1Y 5AS
Tel: (071) 930 8903/4/5
Provides an informed and independent voice on national, regional and environmental planning policies and legislation. Campaigns for more local initiatives and decentralisation.

Urban and Economic Development Group Ltd (URBED)
3 Stamford Street
London SE1 9NT
Tel: (071) 928 9515
Aids community groups in reusing industrial buildings and raising finance.

Volunteer Centre UK
29 Lower Kings Road
Berkhamsted
Herts. HP4 2AB
Tel: (0442) 87 3311
Serves as a national resource agency for everything that concerns volunteers.

Other Useful Addresses

Association of County Councils
Chapter Street
London SW1P 4ND
Tel: (071) 233 6868

Commission for Racial Equality
Elliot House
10-12 Allington Street
London SW1E 5EH
Tel: (071) 828 7022

Community and Youth Workers Union
Unit 202A
The Argent Centre
60 Frederick Street
Birmingham B1 3HS
Tel: (021) 233 2815

Countryside Commission
John Dower House
Crescent Place
Cheltenham
Glos. GL50 3RA
Tel: (0242) 52 1381

Equal Opportunities Commission
Overseas House
Quay Street
Manchester M3 3HN
Tel: (061) 833 9244

Housing Corporation
149 Tottenham Court Road
London W1P OBN
Tel: (071) 387 9466

Local Government Information Unit
1-5 Bath Street
London EC1V 9QQ
Tel: (071) 608 1051

Scottish Council of Voluntary Organisations
18-19 Claremont Crescent
Edinburgh EH7 4HX
Tel: (031) 556 3882

Trades Union Congress
Congress House
Great Russell Street
London WC1B 3LS
Tel: (071) 636 4030

Voluntary Services Unit
50 Queen Anne's Gate
London SW1H 9AT
Tel: (071) 273 2146

Wales Council for Voluntary Action
Llys Ifor, Crescent Road
Caerffili
Mid Glamorgan CF8 1XL
Tel: (0222) 86 9224